PUBLISHER COMMENTARY

There is a reason the U.S. Air Force has one of the best cyberwarfare **weapon system** programs.

This Air Force Instruction (AFI), developed in conjunction with other governing directives, prescribes procedures for the Air Force Cyberspace Defense (ACD) weapon system. It covers cybercrew Initial Qualification Training (IQT), through Mission Qualification Training (MQT), to annual Continuation Training (CT). Requalification Training (RT), and certification requirements. It covers standard operating procedures, crew manning, crew duties, operational objectives, mission planning and preparation, mission go/no-go criteria, sortie duration, maintaining mission and Master Station Logs, required equipment, communications and crew coordination, and debrief guidance. Also discussed is the evaluation criteria for qualifying cybercrew members in the ACD weapon system.

This publication pulls together the 3 volumes of the ACD weapon system.

AFI 17-2ACD Vol. 1	AIR FORCE CYBERSPACE DEFENSE (ACD) TRAINING	27 Apr 2017
AFI 17-2ACD Vol. 2	AIR FORCE CYBERSPACE DEFENSE (ACD) STANDARDIZATION AND EVALUATION	27 Apr 2017
AFI 17-2ACD Vol. 3	AIR FORCE CYBERSPACE DEFENSE (ACD) OPERATIONS AND PROCEDURES	27 Apr 2017

These documents establish procedures for developing, distributing, evaluating and using Air Force training products for qualification training. They provide procedures for crew position evaluation criteria and grading used during performance evaluations on operational cyberspace weapon systems. Topics covered include mission management, mission checks/checklist procedures, crew coordination, emergency procedures and equipment, communications and post-mission activity.

Why buy a book you can download for free? We print this so you don't have to.

Some documents are only distributed in <u>electronic media</u>. Some online docs are missing some pages or the graphics are barely legible. When a new standard is released, an engineer prints it out, punches holes and puts it in a 3-ring binder. While this is not a big deal for a 5 or 10-page document, many cyber documents are over 100 pages and printing a large document is a time-consuming effort. So, an engineer that's paid $75 an hour is spending hours simply printing out the tools needed to do the job. That's time that could be better spent doing engineering. We publish these documents so engineers can focus on what they were hired to do – engineering.

A list of **Cybersecurity Standards** we publish is attached at the end of this document.

BY ORDER OF THE SECRETARY
OF THE AIR FORCE

AIR FORCE INSTRUCTION 17-2ACD
VOLUME 1

27 APRIL 2017

Cyberspace

AIR FORCE CYBERSPACE
DEFENSE (ACD) TRAINING

COMPLIANCE WITH THIS PUBLICATION IS MANDATORY

ACCESSIBILITY: Publications and forms are available on the Publishing website at
www.e-Publishing.af.mil for downloading or ordering

RELEASABILITY: There are no releasability restrictions on this publication

OPR: AF/A3CX/A6CX

Certified by: AF/A3C/A6C
(Brig Gen Kevin B. Kennedy)
Pages: 55

This instruction implements Air Force (AF) Policy Directive (AFPD) 17-2, *Cyberspace Operations*, and references AF Instruction (AFI) 17-202, Volume 1, *Cybercrew Training*. It establishes the minimum AF standards for training and qualifying/certifying personnel for performing crewmember duties on the ACD weapon system. This publication applies to all military and civilian AF personnel, members of the AF Reserve Command (AFRC), Air National Guard (ANG), third-party governmental employee and contractor support personnel in accordance with appropriate provisions contained in memoranda support agreements and AF contracts. The authorities to waive wing/unit level requirements in this publication are identified with a Tier ("T-0, T-1, T-2, T-3") number following the compliance statement. See AFI 33-360, *Publications and Forms Management*, Table 1.1, for a description of the authorities associated with the Tier numbers. Submit requests for waivers through the chain of command to the appropriate Tier waiver approval authority, or alternately, to the Publication OPR for non-tiered compliance items. This instruction requires collecting and maintaining information protected by the Privacy Act of 1974 (5 U.S.C. 552a). System of Records Notices F036 AF PC C, Military Personnel Records System, and OPM/GOVT-1, General Personnel Records, apply. Units may supplement this instruction. All supplements will be coordinated through HQ AFSPC/A2/3/6T prior to publication. Process supplements as shown in AFI 33-360. Major Command (MAJCOM) supplements will be coordinated with USAF A3C/A6C. Guidance provided by the lead major command will contain specific training requirements unique to individual and crew positions. Send recommended changes or comments to HQ USAF/A3C/A6C, 1480 Air Force Pentagon, Washington, DC 20330-1480, through appropriate channels, using AF Form 847, *Recommendation for Change of Publication*. When collecting and maintaining information protect it by the Privacy Act of 1974 authorized by 10 U.S.C. 8013. Ensure that all records created as a result of processes prescribed in this publication are maintained in accordance with AF Manual (AFMAN) 33-363, *Management of Records*, and disposed of in accordance with the AF Records Disposition Schedule (RDS) located in the AF Records Information Management System (AFRIMS). See Attachment 1 for a glossary of references and supporting information.

Chapter 1

GENERAL GUIDANCE

1.1. Training Objectives . This instruction prescribes basic policy and guidance for training United States Air Force Cyberspace Defense (ACD) crewmembers according to AFI 17-202 Volume 1.

1.1.1. The overall objective of the ACD training program is to develop and maintain a high state of readiness for the immediate and effective employment across a full range of military options. Mission readiness and effective employment are achieved through the development and mastery of core competencies for ACD crewmembers.

1.1.2. The secondary objective is to standardize ACD training requirements into a single source document.

1.2. Abbreviations, Acronyms and Terms. See Attachment 1.

1.2.1. For the purposes of this instruction, "certification" denotes a commander's action, whereas qualification denotes a formal Stan/Eval evaluation.

1.2.2. Key words explained.

1.2.2.1. "Will" or "shall" indicates a mandatory requirement.

1.2.2.2. "Should" indicates a preferred, but not mandatory, method of accomplishment.

1.2.2.3. "May" indicates an acceptable or suggested means of accomplishment.

1.2.2.4. "Note" indicates operating procedures, techniques, etc. which are considered essential to emphasize.

1.3. Responsibilities:

1.3.1. Lead Command. Air Force Space Command (AFSPC) is designated lead command for the ACD weapon system and is responsible for establishing and standardizing crewmember training requirements in coordination with all other MAJCOMs. AFSPC/A2/3/6 is authorized to manage all training course requirements and training tasks. AFSPC/A2/3/6 will:

1.3.1.1. Chair an annual Realistic Training Review Board (RTRB) to review training requirements and programs for AF cyberspace units. RTRB participants will include applicable AFSPC active and reserve component representatives. All AF units with assigned ACD cybercrews will be invited to send representatives and inputs. **(T-2)**

1.3.1.2. Process all change requests. **(T-2)**

1.3.2. All user MAJCOMs will:

1.3.2.1. Determine training requirements to fulfill primary (and secondary, if applicable) Designed Operational Capability (DOC) statement missions as well as meet unit tasking.

1.3.2.2. Submit MAJCOM supplements to HQ USAF AF/A3CX/A6CX, through HQ AFSPC/A2/3/6T, for approval during topline coordination of the document. Copies of approved and published supplements will be provided by the issuing office to HQ USAF AF/A3C/A6C, HQ AFSPC/A2/3/6T, and applicable MAJCOM offices of primary responsibility (OPR).

1.3.2.3. Review subordinate unit supplemental instructions and training programs annually.

1.3.3. Wings and groups will:

1.3.3.1. Develop programs to ensure training objectives are met. The top training priority should be to train all designated crewmembers to Mission Ready (MR) / Combat Mission Ready (CMR) status. Assist subordinate squadrons in management of training programs, ensure programs meet unit needs, and provide necessary staff support. AFSPC wing/groups will assist Air Reserve Component (ARC) unit training programs as required or requested in accordance with (IAW) applicable unit support programs, memorandums of agreement, or memorandums of understanding. **(T-2)**

1.3.3.2. Attach Cybercrew Position Indicator (CPI)-6/-8/-B/-D personnel to an operational squadron. See Attachment 4 for CPI explanation and definitions. **(T-2)**

1.3.3.3. Except when otherwise mandated, designate the training level to which each CPI–6/-8/-B/-D will train. Upon request, provide AFSPC/A2/3/6T (through MAJCOM/A3T or equivalent) with a list of Basic Mission Capable (BMC) and MR manning positions. Review programs and manning position designations annually. **(T-2)**

1.3.3.4. Develop additional training requirements and/or programs as necessary to meet unit mission requirements. Units may include these requirements in local training procedures. **(T-2)**

1.3.4. Squadrons (SQ). The SQ/CCs top training priority should be to train all designated crewmembers to BMC or MR/CMR. Squadron supervision will **(T-3)**:

1.3.4.1. Maintain training forms and unit certification documents for all squadron personnel and personnel attached to the squadron for cyberspace operations. Certification documentation will be a summary of certification awarded and signed by the Operations Group (OG)/CC, or SQ/CC. Letters of certification may be maintained via electronic storage. **(T-3)**

1.3.4.2. Ensure adequate continuity and supervision of individual training needs, experience and proficiencies of assigned and attached crewmembers. **(T-3)**

1.3.4.3. Ensure review of training and evaluation records of newly assigned crewmembers and those completing formal training to determine the training required for them to achieve BMC or MR status and to ensure provisions of this volume are met. **(T-3)**

1.3.4.4. Ensure Ready Cybercrew Program (RCP) missions are oriented towards maintaining basic skills or tactical employment simulating conditions anticipated in the unit mission. Provide guidance to ensure only effective RCP missions are logged. **(T-3)**

1.3.4.5. Determine missions and events in which individual BMC crewmembers will maintain certification/qualification. **(T-3)**

1.3.4.6. Determine utilization of BMC crewmembers. **(T-3)**

1.3.4.7. Determine how many and which crewmembers will be awarded special certifications (mission commander, etc.) and qualifications (instructor, etc.) **(T-3)**

1.3.4.8. Assist the wing or group in the development of the unit training programs. **(T-3)**

1.3.4.9. Monitor individual assigned and attached crewmember currencies, proficiencies, and requirements. **(T-3)**

1.3.4.10. Ensure crewmembers participate only in sorties, missions, events, and tasks for which they are prepared, trained, qualified and certified. **(T-3)**

1.3.4.11. Ensure flight commanders or designated representatives monitor quality of training, identify training deficiencies, and advise SQ/CC of additional training needs. **(T-3)**

1.3.4.12. Execute unit-level crewmember certifications described in this instruction. **(T-3)**

1.3.5. Individual crewmembers will:

1.3.5.1. Be responsible for monitoring and completing all training requirements. **(T-3)**

1.3.5.2. Ensure they participate only in operational activities for which they are prepared, trained, qualified and certified. **(T-3)**

1.4. Processing Changes. Process changes using the AF Form 847, IAW AFI 33-360, through local and MAJCOM training channels to USAF/A3C/A6C for approval. **(T-2)**

1.5. Training. Crewmember training is designed to progress a crewmember from Initial Qualification Training (IQT), through Mission Qualification Training (MQT), to annual Continuation Training (CT). Requalification Training (RT), Upgrade Training, and Instructor Training are additional training requirements to the ACD weapon system.

1.5.1. IQT. IQT includes training that will normally be conducted during formal syllabus courses at the Formal Training Unit (FTU). See Chapter 2.

1.5.2. MQT. MQT is a unit-developed training program that upgrades IQT-complete crewmembers to BMC or MR status to accomplish the unit DOC statement mission. See Chapter 3.

1.5.3. All CPI-1/-2/-A/-Z designated positions, to include SQ/CC and SQ/DO positions, should maintain MR status. The OG/CC may designate other CPI-6/B positions not assigned to the squadron as MR. See Attachment 4 for CPI explanation and definitions. **(T-1)**

1.5.4. MR / CMR. MR is a status that denotes a crewmember has received the minimum training required to be certified, current and proficient in all of the primary DOC statement mission requirements of their assigned or attached unit. MR crewmembers will maintain currencies that affect MR status, accomplish all core designated training (missions and events), and all mission related training. Failure to complete required MR training or maintain currencies could result in regression to non-MR (NMR) status unless waived by the approval authority.

1.5.5. BMC. A status that denotes a crewmember is receiving the minimum training required to be familiar with all (and may be certified, current, and proficient in some) of the primary DOC statement mission requirements of their assigned or attached unit.

1.5.5.1. All ACD crew positions not designated as MR-coded positions, are by default BMC-coded positions. BMC-coded positions are assigned to crewmembers with the primary job of performing wing supervision or staff functions directly supporting cyberspace operations (e.g., wing staff, Operations Support Squadron (OSS) personnel, etc.). Many of these crewmembers are required to provide additional capability, either in lieu of or in addition to, the personnel assigned to the operational squadrons. **(T-3)**

1.5.5.2. BMC crewmembers must be able to attain MR status and, if required, certification/qualification in 30 days or less for those missions/events in which they maintain familiarization only. **(T-3)**

1.5.5.3. BMC crewmembers accomplish all mission related training designated by their attached SQ/CC. **(T-3)**

1.5.5.4. BMC crewmembers may participate in any real-world mission in which they are current, proficient, and certified/qualified, without any additional training, with the supervision of an instructor as determined by the SQ/CC.

1.5.5.5. Failure to complete required BMC training will result in regression to non-BMC (N-BMC) status. While N-BMC, SQ/CC will determine missions the crewmembers may perform and ensure an instructor supervises the member during real-world mission. **(T-3)**

1.5.6. Upgrade training is normally accomplished after a crewmember is assigned MR/BMC status and is normally in addition to MR/BMC requirements except for Mission Commander (MC) training.

1.5.6.1. SQ/CCs will select crewmembers for upgrade training. **(T-3)**

1.6. Training Concepts and Policies:

1.6.1. Units will design training programs to achieve the highest degree of readiness consistent with safety and resource availability. Training must balance the need for realism against the expected threat, crew capabilities, and safety. This volume provides training guidelines and polices for use with operational procedures specified in applicable operational publications. **(T-3)**

1.6.2. Design training to achieve mission capability in squadron-tasked roles, maintain proficiency, and enhance mission accomplishment and safety. RCP training missions should emphasize either basic combat skills, or scenarios reflecting procedures and operations based on employment plans, location, current intelligence, and opposition capabilities. Use of procedures and actions applicable to mission scenarios are desired. **(T-3)**

1.6.3. Unless specifically directed, the SQ/CC determines the level of supervision necessary to accomplish the required training. If the mission objectives include introduction to tasks or instruction to correct previous discrepancies, then an instructor is required. **(T-3)**

1.7. Experienced Crewmember Requirements. ACD operators are declared experienced on the weapon system when they meet the requirements in Table 1.1. **(T-3)**

Table 1.1. Experienced Crewmember Requirements.

Position	Declared Experienced (Hours)	Mission Commander (Hours)	Notes
ACD-Operator (ACD-O)	400	N/A	1
ACD Operations Controller (ACD-OC)	400	N/A	
ACD Crew Commander (ACD-CC)	400	800	
ACD Operator, Host-Base Security ACD-O/HBS	400	N/A	
ACD Operator, Incident Response ACD-O/IRO	400	N/A	
ACD-O, Defensive Counter-Cyberspace ACD-O/DCC	400	N/A	
Notes: 1. ACD operators with previous cyberspace weapon system experience are declared experienced when they achieve 300 hours operating the ACD weapon system.			

1.8. RCP Policy and Management:

1.8.1. The RCP training cycle coincides with the government fiscal year and is executed IAW the RCP Tasking Memo (RTM). Each RCP CT status (i.e. BMC/MR) is defined by a total number of RCP missions, broken down into mission types, plus specific qualifications and associated events as determined by HHQ guidance and unit commanders. **(T-3)**

1.8.2. The total number of RCP missions for BMC/MR is the primary factor for maintaining an individual's CT status. The breakout of mission types is provided as a guideline to be followed as closely as possible but minor variances are authorized. Variations in mission types may be used as a basis for regression as directed by the SQ/CC. Certification in a mission is determined by the SQ/CC considering higher headquarters (HHQ) guidance and the individual's capabilities. **(T-3)**

1.8.3. An effective RCP training mission requires accomplishing a tactical mission profile or a building block type mission. Each mission requires successfully completing a majority of the applicable events, as determined by the SQ/CC and Attachment 2. **(T-3)**

1.8.4. Progression from BMC to MR requires:

1.8.4.1. A 1-month look back at the MR mission rate. **(T-3)**

1.8.4.2. Certification/qualification in all core missions and events required at MR. **(T-3)**

1.8.4.3. Confirmation that the progressed crewmember can complete the prorated number of mission and event requirements remaining at MR by the end of the training cycle. **(T-3)**

1.8.4.4. Completion of mission-related training, to include a current certification as applicable to the assigned unit's DOC statement. **(T-3)**

1.8.5. Wing MR and BMC crewmembers will complete the required monthly mission rate. If unable, refer to Regression, paragraph 4.9. **(T-3)**

1.8.6. End of cycle training requirements are based on the crewmember's experience level, as outlined in paragraph 1.7, on the last day of the current training cycle. **(T-3)**

1.9. Training Mission Program Development:

1.9.1. RTM BMC/MR mission and event requirements apply to all BMC and MR crewmembers as well as those carrying special mission certifications/qualifications (see Attachment 2). The standard mission requirements listed in the RTM establish the minimum number of missions per training cycle for BMC and MR levels of training. The RTM takes precedence over this volume and may contain updated requirements, missions, events, or tasks not yet incorporated into Attachment 2. The RTM applies to all ACD crewmembers. **(T-2)**

1.9.2. Non-effective sorties are logged when a training sortie is planned and started, but a majority (51%) of valid training for that type of mission is not accomplished due to system malfunction, power failures, etc. To fully account for all sorties, including those sorties impacted by system malfunctions and power failures, log and report non-effective sorties. **(T-3)**

1.10. Training Records and Reports:

1.10.1. Units will maintain crewmember records for individual training and evaluations IAW:

1.10.1.1. AFI 17-202V1.

1.10.1.2. AFI 17-202V2, *Cybercrew Standardization & Evaluation.*

1.10.1.3. Any additional HHQ supplement to the above mentioned volumes.

1.10.2. Track the following information for all crewmembers (as applicable):

1.10.2.1. Mission-related training (e.g., tactics training, crew resource management training, etc.). **(T-3)**

1.10.2.2. Requirements and accomplishment of individual sorties, mission types, and events cumulatively for the training cycle. **(T-3)**

1.10.2.3. RCP mission requirements and accomplishment using 1-month and 3-month running totals for lookback commensurate with CT status (BMC/MR). **(T-3)**

1.10.2.4. Currencies.

1.11. Crewmember Utilization Policy:

1.11.1. Commanders will ensure wing/group crewmember (CPI-1/-2/-A/-Z) fill authorized positions IAW Unit Manning Documents (UMD) and that crewmember status is properly designated (see Attachment 4 for CPI explanation and definitions) **(T-3).** The overall objective is for crewmembers to perform mission-related duties. Supervisors may assign crewmembers to valid, short-term tasks (escort officer, operational review board (ORB), etc.), but must continually weigh the factors involved, such as level of crewmember tasking, proficiency, currency, and experience. For inexperienced crewmembers in the first year of their initial operational assignment, supervisors should limit non-crewmember duties to those related to unit mission activities. **(T-3)**

1.11.2. Evaluators may be used to instruct any phase of training they are qualified to teach to capitalize on their expertise and experience. If an evaluator is an individual's primary or recommending instructor, the same evaluator shall not administer the associated evaluation. **(T-3)**

1.12. Sortie Allocation and Unit Manpower Guidance:

1.12.1. In general, inexperienced CPI-1/-2/-A/-Z crewmembers should receive priority over experienced crewmembers. Priorities for sortie allocation are as follows:

1.12.1.1. Operational Units. MR CPI-1/-2/-A/-Z, MQT CPI-1/-2/-A/-Z, MR CPI-6/-8/-B/-D, MQT CPI-6/-8/-B/-D, and BMC. **(T-3)**

1.12.2. Units should provide assigned CPI-6/-8/-B/-D crewmembers adequate resources to maintain minimum training requirements. However, CPI-6/-8/-B/-D support will not come at the expense of the squadron's primary mission. **(T-3)**

1.13. Training on Operational Missions. Unless specifically prohibited or restricted by weapons system operating procedures, specific theater operations order (OPORD), or specific HHQ guidance, the OG/CC exercising operational control may approve upgrade, certification/qualification, or special certification/qualification training on operational missions. In order to maximize efficient utilization of training resources, units will take maximum advantage of opportunities to conduct appropriate CT items that may be conveniently suited to concurrent operational mission segments. **(T-3)**

1.14. In-Unit Training Time Limitations:

1.14.1. Comply with the time limitations in Table 1.3. Crewmembers entered in an in-unit training program leading to qualification, requalification, or certification will be dedicated to that training program on a full-time basis. **(T-3)**

1.14.2. Training time start date is the date when the first significant training event (a training event directly contributing to qualification, certification, or upgrade) has begun, or 45-days (90-days for ARC) after being attached or assigned to the unit after completion of the formal school; whichever occurs first. Training time ends with the syllabus completion. **(T-3)**

1.14.3. Units will notify the OG/CC (or equivalent) in writing before the crewmember exceeds upgrade training time limits in Table 1.2. SQ/CCs may extend listed training times up to 60 days (120 days ARC) provided appropriate documentation is included in the training folder. **(T-3)**

1.14.3.1. Include training difficulty, unit corrective action to resolve and prevent recurrence, and estimated completion date. **(T-3)**

Table 1.2. In-Unit Training Time Limitations (Calendar Days). (T-3).

Training	Crew Commander	Operations Controller	Operator	Notes
MQT	90	90	90	1, 3
RT	45	45	45	1, 3
Mission Certification	30	30	30	1, 3
Instructor Upgrade	45	45	45	1, 3
Position Upgrade	60	60	60	1, 3
Special Mission Upgrade	60	60	60	1, 3
BMC to MR	30	30	30	1, 2, 3
Notes:				
1. Training time begins with the first training event				
2. BMC crewmembers must be able to attain MR status and, if required, certification / qualification in 30 days or less for those missions/events that they maintain familiarization only				
3. 180 days for non-full time ARC/ANG members				

1.15. Periodic and End-of-Cycle Training Reports.

1.15.1. Periodic Reporting. Squadrons will submit a periodic training report to MAJCOM/A3TT (or equivalent) quarterly. Reports will consist of a SQ/CC memo summarizing previous report results/issues, current training plan summary and significant shortfalls/limiting factors (LIMFACS) affecting training. **(T-3)**

1.15.2. End-of-Cycle Reporting. Squadrons will submit an End-of-Cycle Training Report to MAJCOM/A3TT (or equivalent) NLT 15 October. Report all deviations from the training requirements in this volume or the RTM, after proration at the end of the training cycle. **(T-3)**

1.16. Waiver Authority:

1.16.1. Waivers. Unless another approval authority is cited ("T-0, T-1, T-2, T-3"), waiver authority for this volume is the MAJCOM/A3 (or equivalent). Submit requests for waivers using AF Form 679 through the chain of command to the appropriate Tier waiver approval authority.   If approved, waivers remain in effect for the life of the published guidance, unless the waiver authority specifies a shorter period of time, cancels in writing, or issues a change that alters the basis for the waiver.

1.16.2. With MAJCOM/A3 (or equivalent) approval, waiver authority for all requirements of the RTM is the OG/CC. Additional guidance may be provided in the memo. Unless specifically noted otherwise in the appropriate section, and also with MAJCOM/A3 (or equivalent) approval, the OG/CC may adjust individual requirements in Chapter 4 and Chapter 5, on a case-by-case basis, to accommodate variations in crewmember experience and performance. **(T-2)**

1.16.3. Formal School Training and Prerequisites. Any planned exception to a formal course syllabus (or prerequisite) requires a syllabus waiver. Submit waiver request through MAJCOM/A3T (or equivalent) to the waiver authority listed in the course syllabus. If required for units' designated mission, events waived or not accomplished at the formal school will be accomplished in-unit before assigning MR status. **(T-2)**

1.16.4. In-Unit Training Waiver. MAJCOM/A3T (or equivalent) is approval/waiver authority for in-unit training to include syllabus and prerequisite waivers. Before approval, review the appropriate syllabus and consider availability of formal instruction and requirements. All in-unit training will utilize formal courseware in accordance with AFI 17-202V1. MAJCOMs will coordinate with the FTU to arrange courseware delivery to the unit for in-unit training. **(T-2)**

1.16.5. Waiver authority for supplemental guidance will be as specified in the supplement and approved through higher level coordination authority. **(T-2)**

1.16.6. Units subordinate to a NAF will forward requests through the NAF/A3T (or equivalent) to the MAJCOM/A3T (or equivalent). Waivers from other than the MAJCOM/A3 (or equivalent) will include the appropriate MAJCOM/A3 (or equivalent) as an information addressee. (T-2)

Chapter 2

INITIAL QUALIFICATION TRAINING

2.1. General. This chapter outlines ACD IQT requirements for all crewmembers.

2.2. Formal Training. ACD IQT includes training that will normally be conducted during formal syllabus courses at the FTU.

2.3. Local Training. When FTU training is not available within a reasonable time period, local IQT may be performed at the unit IAW the provisions of this chapter. Local IQT will be conducted using appropriate formal training course syllabus and requirements. When local IQT is authorized, the gaining unit is responsible for providing this training. **(T-2)**

 2.3.1. Requests to conduct local IQT will include the following:

  2.3.1.1. Justification for the local training in lieu of FTU training. **(T-2)**

  2.3.1.2. Summary of individual's mission related experience, to include dates. **(T-2)**

  2.3.1.3. Date training will begin and expected completion date. **(T-2)**

  2.3.1.4. Requested exceptions to formal course syllabus, with rationale. **(T-2)**

2.4. Mission-Related Training. Mission-related training may be tailored to the individual's background and experience or particular local conditions. Current and available reference materials, such as AFTTP 3-1.ACD, other applicable AFTTP 3-1s and 3-3s, unit guides, and other available training material and programs, will be used as supporting materials to the maximum extent possible. **(T-3)**

2.5. Mission Training:

 2.5.1. Mission sequence and prerequisites will be IAW the appropriate formal course syllabus (unless waived). **(T-2)**

 2.5.2. Training will be completed within the time specified by the syllabus. Failure to complete within the specified time limit requires notification through channels to MAJCOM/A3 with crewmember's name, rank, reason for delay, planned actions, and estimated completion date. **(T-2)**

 2.5.3. Crewmembers in IQT will train under the supervision of an instructor as annotated in the formal course syllabus until completing the INIT QUAL evaluation. **(T-3)**

 2.5.4. Formal course syllabus mission objectives and tasks are minimum requirements for IQT. However, additional training events, based on student proficiency and background, may be incorporated into the IQT program with SQ/CC authorization. Additional training due to student non-progression is available within the constraints of the formal course syllabus and may be added at SQ/CC discretion. **(T-3)**

2.6. IQT for Senior Officers:

 2.6.1. All senior officer training (colonel selects and above) will be conducted at the FTUs unless waived IAW AFI 17-202V1. **(T-2)**

2.6.2. Senior officers must meet course entry prerequisites and will complete all syllabus requirements unless waived IAW AFI 17-202V1. **(T-2)**

2.6.3. If senior officers are trained at the base to which they are assigned they will be considered in a formal training status for the duration of the course. Their duties will be delegated to appropriate deputy commanders or vice commanders until training is completed. Waiver authority for this paragraph is MAJCOM/CC (submitted through MAJCOM/A3). **(T-2)**

Chapter 3

MISSION QUALIFICATION AND CERTIFICATION TRAINING

3.1. General. MQT is a unit-developed training program that upgrades IQT-complete crewmembers to BMC or MR status to accomplish the unit DOC statement missions. Guidance in this chapter, which represents the minimum, is provided to assist SQ/CCs in developing their MQT program, which must have OG/CC approval prior to use. Squadrons may further tailor their program for individual crewmembers, based on current qualifications (e.g., USAFWS graduate, Instructor), certifications (e.g., mission commander (MC), defensive counter-cyberspace (DCC), Stan/Eval), experience, currency, documented performance, and formal training. Squadrons may use applicable portions of MQT to create a recertification program for crewmembers who regress from MR to BMC status. **(T-3)**

3.1.1. MQT will be completed within 90 calendar days starting from the crewmember's first duty day in the gaining unit. If the crewmember elects to take leave prior to being entered into MQT, the timing will begin after the termination of the leave. Training is complete upon SQ/CC certification of BMC/MR status (subsequent to the successful completion of the MQT mission qualification evaluation (MSN)). Notify MAJCOM/A3T (through MAJCOM/A3TT or equivalent) either if training exceeds the 90-day time period or there is a delay beginning MQT (e.g., due to security clearance) that exceeds 30 days. For ARC crewmembers, MQT will start within 90 days from competing IQT. **(T-3)**

3.2. Mission-Related Training:

3.2.1. Units will develop blocks of instruction covering areas pertinent to the mission as determined by the SQ/CC. Training accomplished during IQT may be credited towards this requirement. **(T-3)**

3.2.2. Mission-related training may be tailored to the individual's background and experience or particular local conditions. Current and available reference materials, such as AFTTP 3-1.ACD, other applicable AFTTP 3-1s and 3-3s, unit guides, and other available training material and programs, will be used as supporting materials to the maximum extent possible. **(T-3)**

Table 3.1. Mission-Related Training Requirements.

Code	Event	Crew Position	Notes
GTR001	Unit Indoctrination Training	All	1
GTR002	Weapons and Tactics	All	1
GTR003	Risk Management	All	1, 2
Notes:			
1. Accomplish upon arrival after each permanent change of station. See Attachment 2 for event description.			
2. Previously trained crewmembers transferring between units need to re-accomplish this event if they have lost currency or as determined by the SQ/CC.			

3.2.3. Mission-related training will be built to support the mission and concept of operations of the individual squadron; incorporate appropriate portions of AF Tactics, Techniques, and Procedures (AFTTP) 3-1.ACD and other mission-related documents. **(T-3)**

3.3. Initial Certification:

3.3.1. Initial Certification of MR crewmembers will be completed within 30 days after completing MQT (recommended, but not required for BMC crewmembers). Failure to comply will result in regression to NMR until complete. Suggested briefing guides are at Attachment 3. Each crewmember will demonstrate to a formal board a satisfactory knowledge of the squadron's primary DOC statement missions. The purpose of this board is to act as final check before certifying a crewmember as MR. Board composition will be established by the SQ/CC. Desired composition is SQ/CC or SQ/DO (chairman), weapons and tactics, training, intelligence, and other mission-area expert representatives. **(T-3)**

3.4. Mission Training:

3.4.1. At SQ/CC discretion, applicable missions from those listed below will be used to build the local MQT program. MQT programs should use profiles typical of squadron missions. **(T-3)**

3.4.2. Supervision. A SQ instructor is required for all training missions unless specified otherwise. **(T-3)**

3.4.3. Minimum Sortie Requirements. The minimum sorties required in a local MQT program will be IAW the MQT course syllabus (not required if portions of the MQT program are used to recertify crewmembers that regress from MR to BMC). **(T-3)**

3.4.4. Mission sequence and prerequisites will be IAW the appropriate unit MQT course syllabus (unless waived). **(T-3)**

3.4.5. Mission Objectives: Be familiar with local area requirements and procedures. Specific Mission Tasks: local area familiarization, emergency procedures, other tasks and as determined. **(T-3)**

3.4.6. Individual events may be accomplished anytime during MQT, however all events will be accomplished prior to SQ/CC certification of BMC/MR status. **(T-3)**

3.4.7. Training will be completed within the time specified by the syllabus. Failure to complete within the specified time limit requires notification through channels to the MAJCOM/A3T with crewmember's name, rank, reason for delay, planned actions, and estimated completion date. **(T-2)**

3.4.8. Crewmembers in MQT will train under the appropriate supervision as annotated in the formal course syllabus until completing the MSN evaluation. **(T-3)**

3.4.9. Formal course syllabus mission objectives and tasks are minimum requirements for MQT. However, additional training events, based on student proficiency and background, may be incorporated into the MQT program with SQ/CC authorization. Additional training due to student non-progression is available within the constraints of the formal course syllabus and may be added at SQ/CC discretion. **(T-3)**

3.5. MQT for Senior Officers:

3.5.1. All senior officer training (colonel selects and above) will be conducted at the unit. **(T-2)**

3.5.2. Senior officers must meet course entry prerequisites and will complete all syllabus requirements unless waived by the MAJCOM/A3. **(T-2)**

3.5.3. Senior officers will be considered in a formal training status for the duration of the course.   Their duties will be turned over to appropriate deputy commanders or vice commanders until training is completed. Waiver authority for this paragraph is the MAJCOM/CC (submitted through the MAJCOM/A3). **(T-2)**

Chapter 4

CONTINUATION TRAINING

4.1. General. This chapter establishes the minimum crewmember training requirements to maintain BMC or MR for an assigned training status. The SQ/CC will ensure each crewmember receives sufficient training to maintain individual currency and proficiency **(T-3)**.

4.2. Crewmember Status. SQ/CCs will assign ACD crewmembers a status using the following criteria:

4.2.1. Mission Ready (MR). A status that denotes a crewmember received the minimum training required to be certified, current, and proficient in all of the primary DOC statement mission requirements of their assigned or attached unit.

4.2.2. Non-Mission Ready (NMR). A crewmember that is unqualified, non-current or incomplete in required continuation training, or not certified to perform the unit mission.

4.2.3. Basic Mission Capable (BMC). A crewmember who satisfactorily completed IQT and MQT, but is not fully-certified to MR status.

4.2.3.1. The crewmember shall be able to attain full unit mission certification to meet operational tasking within 30 days. **(T-3)**

4.2.3.2. The OG/CC may define a portion of the unit's operational mission and declare an assigned or attached crewmember MR if all training requirements for that part of the operational mission are met. The crewmember does not need to attain full mission certification unless directed by the OG/CC. **(T-3)**

4.2.4. MR and BMC crewmembers will accomplish and/or maintain RCP requirements, for their respective status, and the appropriate events in the RCP tables in this Instruction and the RTM. **(T-3)**

4.3. Training Events/Tables. Standardized training events identifiers and descriptions are located in Attachment 2. Units will include unit-specific events to include a description in their local training documentation. **(T-3)**

4.3.1. Crediting Event Accomplishment. Credit events accomplished on training, operational missions and satisfactory evaluations or certifications toward RCP requirements and establish a subsequent due date. Use date of successful evaluation as the date of accomplishment for all mission-related training events that were trained during a formal course. A successful evaluation establishes a new current and qualified reference date for all accomplished events. For training during IQT or requalification training, numbers of events accomplished prior to the evaluation are not credited to any crew position. In all cases, numbers of events successfully accomplished during the evaluation or certification are credited toward the crew position. **(T-3)**

4.3.2. For an unsatisfactory evaluation, do not log CT requirements for those events graded U/Q3 (according to AFI 17-202V2) until re-qualified. **(T-3)**

4.3.3. Instructors and evaluators may credit up to 50 percent of their total CT requirements while instructing or evaluating. **(T-3)**

4.4. Continuation Training Requirements. Completion and tracking of continuation training is ultimately the responsibility of the individual crewmember. Crewmembers should actively work with their supervisors, unit schedulers and training offices to ensure accomplishment of their continuation training requirements. **(T-3)**

4.4.1. Mission-Related Training Events. Crewmembers will comply with requirements of Table 4.1. Failure to accomplish events in Table 4.1 leads to NMR status. **(T-3)**

4.4.2. Weapons and Tactics Academic Training. Units will establish a weapons and tactics academic training program to satisfy MQT and CT requirements. Training is required semi-annually during each training cycle. SQ/CCs will provide guidance to unit weapons shops to ensure all crewmembers are informed/reminded of new/current ACD weapons, systems, and mission-specific TTPs. The program will require successful completion of an open book examination (80 percent minimum to pass). Unit training offices will track completion of tactics training. Failure to attend tactics training will result in NMR status. **(T-3)**

4.4.3. Instruction and tests should include (as applicable), but are not limited to:

4.4.3.1. Applicable AF Tactics, Techniques, and Procedure (AFTTP) 3-1 & 3-3 series publications, AFI 17-2ACD Volume 3, and other documents pertaining to the execution of the unit's mission. **(T-3)**

4.4.3.2. Specialized training to support specific weapons, tactics, mission capabilities, rules of engagement (ROE), and other mission related activities. **(T-3)**

4.4.4. CT Certification. CT Certification updates crew members on their squadron's wartime mission. Each MR crew member will participate in a squadron CT certification as a briefer, board member, or participant every 18 months. BMC crew members should participate in a CT Certification to facilitate future upgrade to MR status, at the discretion of the SQ/CC. Crew members who participate on the certification board receive credit for CT Certification. **(T-3)**

4.4.5. Risk Management (RM). Crew members will participate in RM training once every training cycle. Briefings will include the concepts outlined in AFPAM 90-803, Risk Management (RM) Guidelines and Tools. Unit training offices will track RM training. Failure to attend RM training will result in NMR status. **(T-3)**

Table 4.1. ACD Crew Mission-Related CT Requirements.

Code	Event	Position	Frequency	Notes
GTR001	Weapons & Tactics	All	179d	1, 3
GTR002	Certification	All	18m	2, 3
GTR003	Risk Management	All	365d	1, 3
Notes:				
1. "d" is the maximum number of days between events.				
2. "m" is the maximum number of months between events.				
3. Failure to complete this event within the time prescribed leads to NMR status. Crewmembers will not be able to accomplish unsupervised crew duties until the delinquent event is accomplished or waived.				

4.4.6. Mission Training Events. Crewmembers will comply with requirements of the RTM for their respective position. Total sorties and events are minimums which ensure training to continually meet all DOC tasked requirements and may not be reduced except in proration/waiver. Unless specifically noted the OG/CC is the waiver authority for all RCP requirements and for all provisions in Chapter 4 and Chapter 5 of this volume. Failure to accomplish events in these tables may lead to NMR status. **(T-3)**

4.5. Specialized Mission Training. Training in any special skills (e.g., tactics, weapon system capabilities, responsibilities, etc.) necessary to carry out the unit's assigned mission that is not required by every crewmember. Specialized training consists of upgrade training such as instructor etc., as well as CT to maintain certification, currency, and proficiency in unit tasked special capabilities and missions. **(T-3)**

4.5.1. Specialized training is normally accomplished after a crewmember is assigned MR/BMC status and is normally in addition to MR/BMC requirements except for Mission Commander (MC) training. Unless otherwise specified, crewmembers in MR or BMC positions may hold special mission certifications as long as any additional training requirements are accomplished. (See Chapter 5) **(T-3)**

4.5.2. The SQ/CC will determine and assign crewmembers that will train for and maintain special mission qualifications and certifications. **(T-3)**

4.6. Multiple Qualification/Currency. See AFI 17-202V1, AFI 17-202V2, applicable HHQ guidance, and AFI 17-2ACD Volume 2, *Air Force Cyberspace Defense (ACD) Standardization and Evaluation*, for multiple qualifications.

4.6.1. Multiple qualifications are not appropriate for senior wing supervisors (OG/CD and above). **(T-2)**

4.6.2. Multiple Requirements. Crewmembers will satisfy at least 50 percent of the sortie requirements in their primary weapon system. If MR, they will meet all RCP mission and event requirements of the primary weapon system. **(T-3)**

4.6.3. Multiple Currencies. Crewmembers will conduct a sortie at least once each 45 days (90 days for ARC crewmembers) in each weapon system. They will comply with all other currency requirements for each weapon system. **(T-3)**

4.6.4. Multiple qualified crewmembers must complete training IAW the approved syllabus for each weapon system. **(T-3)**

4.7. Currencies, Proficiency and Requalification.

4.7.1. Currency. The RTM defines currency requirements for BMC/MR crewmembers. Crewmembers may not instruct, evaluate or perform any event in which they are not qualified and current unless under instructor supervision. Currency may be established or updated by:

4.7.1.1. Accomplishing the event as a qualified crewmember provided member's currency has not expired. **(T-3)**

4.7.1.2. Accomplishing the event as a qualified crewmember under supervision of a current instructor. **(T-3)**

4.7.1.3. Satisfactorily performing events on any evaluation. **(T-3)**

4.7.2. If a crewmember loses a specific currency, thereby requiring recurrency, that mission or event may not be performed except for the purpose of regaining currency. Non-current events must be satisfied before the crewmember is considered certified/qualified (as applicable) to perform those events unsupervised. Loss of currencies affecting MR status require regression to NMR (see paragraph 4.9); loss of currencies not affecting MR status does not require regression. **(T-3)**

4.8. Loss of Instructor Status and Requalification/Recurrency.

4.8.1. Instructors may lose instructor status for the following:

4.8.1.1. Loss of currency for more than 180 days. **(T-3)**

4.8.1.2. Instructors become noncurrent in a mission or event which causes removal from MR/BMC status and the SQ/CC deems that loss of currency is of sufficient importance to require complete decertification (but not a complete loss of qualification). **(T-3)**

4.8.1.2.1. As long as the affected crewmember retains instructor qualification IAW AFI 17-202V2, recertification will be at the SQ/CC's discretion. **(T-3)**

4.8.1.2.2. If the SQ/CC does not elect to decertify the individual or if the individual becomes noncurrent in missions or events which do not require removal from MR status, instructor status may be retained, but the instructor will not instruct that mission or event until the required currency is regained. **(T-3)**

4.8.2. Instructor Lack of Ability. Instructors serve solely at the discretion of the SQ/CC. Instructors should exemplify a higher level of performance and present themselves as reliable and authoritative experts in their respective duty positions. Instructors exhibiting substandard performance should be reviewed for suitability of continued instructor duty. **(T-3)** Instructors will be decertified if:

4.8.2.1. Awarded a less than fully qualified grade in any area of the evaluation regardless of overall crewmember position qualification. **(T-3)**

4.8.2.2. They fail an evaluation. **(T-3)**

4.8.2.3. The SQ/CC deems the instructor is substandard, ineffective, or providing incorrect procedures, techniques, or policy guidance. **(T-3)**

4.8.2.4. Decertified instructors may regain instructor status by correcting applicable deficiencies and completing the training and/or evaluation as specified by the SQ/CC. **(T-3)**

4.9. Regression.

4.9.1. BMC/MR Regression for Failure to Meet Lookback. Only RCP training missions and cyberspace operations sorties may be used for lookback. If a crewmember does not meet lookback requirements throughout the training cycle, SQ/CC can: regress the crewmember to NMR/N-BMC, as applicable, or remove the crewmember from a BMC/MR manning position. **(T-3)**

4.9.1.1. Failure to meet 1-month lookback requires a review of the crewmember's 3-month sortie history. If the 3-month lookback is met, the crewmember may, at SQ/CC discretion, remain in MR/BMC status. Failure to meet the 3-month lookback will result in regression to NMR/N-BMC, as applicable, or the crewmember may be placed in probation status for 1 month at the SQ/CC's discretion. If probation is chosen, the only way to remove a crewmember from probation and preserve the current status is to reestablish a 1-month lookback at the end of the probation period. **(T-3)**

4.9.1.2. Lookback computations begin following completion of MQT. The crewmember must maintain 1-month lookback until 3-month lookback is established. SQ/CCs may apply probation rules as described in paragraph 4.9.1.1 if a new MR/BMC crewmember fails to meet 1-month lookback while establishing 3-month lookback. In addition, 1-month lookback will start the first full month of MR/BMC status. **(T-3)**

4.9.2. Regression for Failed Evaluations. Crewmembers who fail a periodic evaluation are unqualified and will regress to NMR/N-BMC as applicable. Crewmembers will remain NMR/N-BMC until they have successfully completed required corrective action, re-evaluation, and are re-certified by the SQ/CC. **(T-3)**

4.9.3. Failure to Maintain Standards. If a qualified crewmember demonstrates lack of proficiency or knowledge the SQ/CC may elect to regress the individual to NMR/M-BMC as applicable. These crewmembers will remain NMR/N-BMC until successful completion of corrective action as determined by the SQ/CC, an evaluation if required and are re-certified by the SQ/CC. **(T-3)**

4.10. End of Cycle Requirements. Crewmembers who fail to complete mission or event requirements by the end of training cycle may require additional training depending on the type and magnitude of the deficiency. Refer to paragraph 4.11 for proration guidance. In all cases, units will report training shortfalls to the OG/CC. **(T-3)**

4.10.1. Crewmembers failing to meet annual RCP events or minimum total sortie requirements may continue CT at MR/BMC as determined by lookback. The SQ/CC will determine if additional training is required. **(T-3)**

4.10.2. Failure to meet specific BMC and MR mission type requirements will result in one of the following:

4.10.2.1. Regression to NMR/N-BMC if the SQ/CC determines the mission type deficiency is significant. To regain MR/BMC, the crewmember will complete all deficient mission types. These missions may also be counted toward the total requirements for the new training cycle. **(T-3)**

4.10.2.2. Continuation at BMC/MR if total RCP missions and lookback are maintained and the mission type deficiencies are deemed insignificant by the SQ/CC. The SQ/CC will determine if any additional training is required to address shortfalls. **(T-3)**

4.10.3. Failure to accomplish missions/events required for Special Mission capabilities or certifications/qualifications will result in loss of that certification/qualification. The SQ/CC will determine recertification requirements. Requalification requirements are IAW AFI 17-202V2, applicable HHQ guidance, and AFI 17-2ACD V2. **(T-3)**

4.11. Proration of Training.

4.11.1. Proration of End-of-Cycle Requirements. At the end of the training cycle the SQ/CC may prorate any training requirements precluded by the following events: initial arrival date in squadron, emergency leave, non-mission temporary duty (TDY) (i.e., PME) or exercises, or deployments. Ordinary annual leave will not be considered as non-availability. Other extenuating circumstances, as determined by the SQ/CC, that prevent crewmembers from mission duties for more than 15 consecutive days may be considered as non-availability for proration purposes. The following guidelines apply:

4.11.1.1. Proration will not be used to mask training or planning deficiencies. **(T-3)**

4.11.1.2. Proration is based on cumulative days of non-availability for mission duties in the training cycle. Use Table 4.2 to determine the number of months to be prorated based on each period of cumulative non-mission duty calendar days. **(T-3)**

4.11.1.3. If IQT or MQT is re-accomplished, a crewmember's training cycle will start over at a prorated share following completion of IQT/MQT. **(T-3)**

4.11.1.4. No requirement may be prorated below one month. Prorated numbers resulting in fractions of less than 0.5 month will be rounded to the next lower whole number (one or greater). **(T-3)**

4.11.1.5. Newly assigned crewmembers achieving MR/BMC after the 15th of the month are considered to be in CT on the first day of the following month for proration purposes. A prorated share of RCP missions must be completed in CT. **(T-3)**

4.11.1.6. A crewmember's last month on station prior to departing PCS may be prorated provided 1 month's proration is not exceeded. Individuals departing PCS may be considered MR for reporting purposes during a period of 60 days from date of last mission/sortie, or until loss of MR currency, port call date, or sign in at new duty station, whichever occurs first. **(T-3)**

4.11.1.7. MR crewmembers who attend the USAFWS in TDY-and-return status may be reported throughout the TDY as MR. Upon return, those crewmembers will accomplish a prorated share of mission and event requirements. **(T-3)**

4.12. Operational Missions. The following procedures are intended to provide flexibility in accomplishing the unit's CT program. Sorties conducted in support of operations will be logged and count toward annual RCP requirements for lookback purposes. Operational missions and events may be used to update proficiency/currency requirements if they meet the criteria in Attachment 2. **(T-3)**

4.12.1. Example: Capt Jones was granted 17 days of emergency leave in January and attended SOS in residence from March through April for 56 consecutive calendar days. The SQ/CC authorized a total of two months proration from his training cycle (two months for the 73 cumulative days of non-availability).

Table 4.2. Proration Allowance.

CUMULATIVE DAYS OF NON-MISSION ACTIVITY	PRORATION ALLOWED (Months)
0 – 15	0
16 – 45	1
46 – 75	2
76 – 105	3
106 – 135	4
136 – 165	5
166 – 195	6
196 – 225	7
226 – 255	8
256 – 285	9
286 – 315	10
316 – 345	11
Over 345	12

4.13. Regaining BMC/MR Status.

4.13.1. If MR/BMC status is lost due to failure to meet the end of cycle event requirements, re-certification/re-qualification is IAW paragraph 4.10. **(T-3)**

4.13.2. If MR/BMC status is lost due to failure to meet lookback IAW paragraph 4.10, the following applies (timing starts from the date the crewmember was removed from MR/BMC status):

4.13.2.1. Up to 90 Days. Complete a SQ/CC approved recertification program (documented in the individual's training folder) to return the crewmember to MR/BMC standards. Upon completion of the recertification program, the MR/BMC crewmember must also meet the subsequent 1-month lookback requirement prior to reclaiming MR/BMC status. The missions and events accomplished during the recertification program may be credited towards their total/type mission and event requirements for the training cycle as well as for their monthly mission requirement. In addition, all RCP event currencies must be regained. The SQ/CC will approve any other additional training prior to MR recertification. **(T-3)**

4.13.2.2. 91-180 Days. Same as above, plus open/closed book qualification examinations (IAW AFI 17-202V2). Open/closed book exams will be documented IAW AFI 17-202V2. **(T-3)**

4.13.2.3. 181 Days and Beyond. Reaccomplish a SQ/CC-directed MQT program to include a formal MSN evaluation IAW AFI 17-202V2, applicable HHQ guidance, and AFI 17-2ACD V2. **(T-3)**

Figure 4.1. Regression Flow Chart

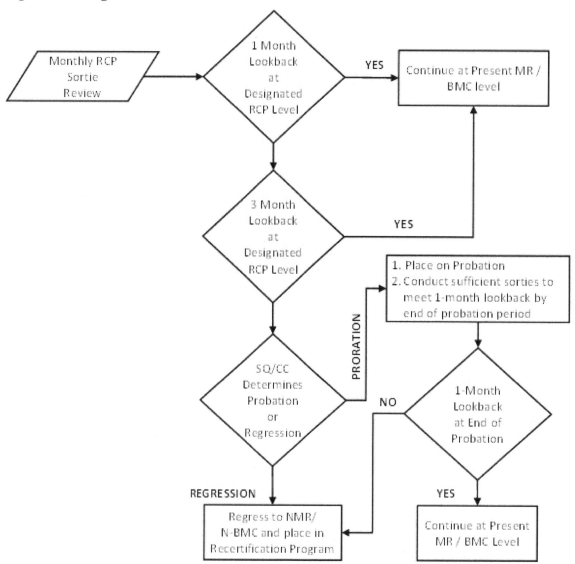

Chapter 5

UPGRADE TRAINING

5.1. General. This chapter outlines duties and responsibilities for units to upgrade, certify, and maintain currency/proficiency for special missions and certifications/qualifications. SQ/CCs may tailor programs for individuals based on previous experience, qualifications, and documented performance. These capabilities and certifications/qualifications are in addition to unit core missions and do not apply to every crewmember assigned or attached to the unit.

5.2. Commanders must ensure each candidate has the ability, judgment, technical expertise, skill, and experience when selecting a crewmember for upgrade or specialized mission training. **(T-2)**

Table 5.1. Minimum Upgrade Training Requirements.

Upgrading From	Upgrading To	Prerequisites	Tasks & Events to Complete Upgrade
ACD Operator	ACD DCC	Experienced ACD-O, Advanced Cyberspace Training	DCC related tasks, Evaluation
ACD Operator	ACD HBS	Experienced ACD-O, DISA HBS Training	HBS related tasks, Evaluation
ACD Operator	ACD IR	Experienced ACD-O, Encase Training	IR related tasks, Evaluation
ACD Operator	ACD Ops Controller	Experienced IR, DCC, or HBS	Cyberspace Ops Controller Upgrade training, Evaluation
ACD Operator	ACD Crew CC	Experienced IR, DCC, or HBS	Cyberspace Crew Commander Upgrade training, Evaluation
ACD Crew CC	Mission CC	Experienced ACD-CC	SQ/CC certification Wing Mission Commander Course
Any Position	Instructor	Experienced (any position); Instructor Training Course	Instructor Qual & SQ/CC certification

5.3. Instructor Upgrade. This section establishes the minimum guidelines for instructor upgrade.

5.3.1. Instructor Responsibilities. An AF instructor shall be a subject matter expert adept in the methodology of instruction. The instructor shall be proficient in evaluating, diagnosing, and critiquing student performance, identifying learning objectives and difficulties, and prescribing and conducting remedial instruction. The instructor must be able to conduct instruction in all training venues (e.g., classroom, training devices, ops floor, mission execution, etc.) **(T-3)**

5.3.1.1. Instructor Prerequisites. SQ/CCs will consider ability, judgment, technical expertise, skill, and experience when selecting a crewmember for instructor upgrade. **(T-3)**

5.3.1.2. For instructor minimum requirements, see Table 5.1. All instructor candidates will be MR in their unit's mission. **(T-3)**

Table 5.2. Instructor Upgrade Requirements.

Position	Instructor	Evaluator	Tasks/Events to Complete Upgrade	Notes
ACD	800	1000	Instructor Training Course Instructor Qualification Evaluation SQ/CC certification	See Notes 1 & 2
Notes: 1. Instructor training must meet all AFI 17-202 V1 and other HHQ guidance requirements 2. Award of the "K" prefix will be IAW AF Officer and Enlisted Classification Directories				

5.3.1.3. Training. Instructor training should expand the instructor candidate's weapon-system subject matter expertise. Instructor training will include methodology of instruction and make instructor candidates proficient in evaluating, diagnosing, and critiquing student performance, identifying learning objectives and difficulties, and prescribing and conducting remedial instruction. The instructor candidate must be able to conduct instruction in all training venues (e.g., classroom, training devices, ops floor, mission execution, etc.). **(T-3)**

5.3.1.4. Testing. Units will develop tests based on the training requirements in AFI 17-202V1, HHQ Supplements, this publication, and other relevant guidance. The test will be closed book and consist of a minimum of 25 questions. To receive credit for this training each instructor candidate must pass the test with a minimum score of 80 percent. Units will develop and maintain an instructor test master question file. **(T-3)**

5.3.1.5. Qualification and Certification. All instructor candidates will demonstrate to an evaluator their ability to instruct and perform selected tasks and items according to applicable directives. Following successful completion of instructor training and evaluation, the SQ/CC or designated representative will personally interview the candidate and review instructor responsibilities, scope of duties, authority, and philosophy. SQ/CC will certify a new instructor by placing a letter of certification in the training folder and indicate qualifications on a Letter of Certification. **(T-3)**

5.4. Mission Commander (MC). This section establishes the minimum guidelines for MC training.

5.4.1. Responsibilities. The MC is responsible for planning, coordinating, briefing, executing, and debriefing cyberspace large force employment packages. MCs, once certified, are authorized to lead wing-level composite force missions. **(T-3)**

5.4.2. MC Prerequisites. SQ/CCs will consider ability, judgment, technical expertise, skill, and experience when selecting a crewmember for MC upgrade. **(T-3)**

5.4.2.1. Minimum MC requirements are an experienced ACD crew commander with 12 months MR status. **(T-3)**

5.4.3. Training. Wings will develop and maintain a Mission Commander Course. MCs must satisfactorily complete a Mission Commander Course prior to MC certification. **(T-3)**

5.4.4. Mission Execution. As a minimum, the upgrading MC will observe a certified MC during the planning, briefing, flight, and debrief of at least one composite force mission. Prior to certification, the MC candidate will plan, brief, execute, and debrief (PBED) a minimum of one rehearsal of concept (ROC) large force exercise (LFE) under instructor supervision. **(T-3)**

5.4.5. Certification. Following successful completion of MC training, the SQ/CC or designated representative will personally interview the candidate and review MC responsibilities, scope of duties, authority, and philosophy. SQ/CC will certify a new MC by placing a letter of certification in the training folder and indicate qualifications on a Letter of Certification. **(T-3)**

WILLIAM J. BENDER, Lt Gen, USAF
Chief of Information Dominance and Chief
Information Officer

Attachment 1

GLOSSARY OF REFERENCES AND SUPPORTING INFORMATION

References

AFPD 17-2, *Cyberspace Operations*, 12 April 2016

AFI 17-202 Volume 1, *Cybercrew Training*, 2 April 2014

AFI 17-202 Volume 2, *Cybercrew Standardization and Evaluation Program*, 15 October 2014

AFI 17-2ACD Volume 2, *Air Force Cyberspace Defense (ACD) Standardization and Evaluation*

AFI 33-360, *Publications and Forms Management*, 1 December 2015

AFMAN 33-363, *Management of Records*, 1 March 2008

AFPAM 90-803, *Risk Management (RM) Guidelines and Tools*, 11 February 2013

Privacy Act of 1974 (5 United States Code [U.S.C.] 552a)

Prescribed Forms

None

Adopted Forms

AF Form 847, *Recommendation for Change of Publication*

Abbreviations and Acronyms

ACD—Air Force Cyberspace Defense

ACD-O – Air Force Cyber Defense Operator

ACD-OC – Air Force Cyber Defense Operations Controller

ACD-O/HBS – Air Force Cyber Defense Operator/Host Based Security

ACD-O/IRO – Air Force Cyber Defense Operator/Incident Response

ACD-O/DCC – Air Force Cyber Defense Operator/Defensive Counter Cyberspace

ADO—Assistant Director of Operations

AF—Air Force

AFI—Air Force Instruction

AFMAN—Air Force Manual

AFPD—Air Force Policy Document

AFRC—Air Force Reserve Command

AFRIMS—Air Force Records Information Management System

AFSPC—Air Force Space Command

AFTTP—Air Force Tactics, Techniques and Procedures

ANG—Air National Guard

AOP—ACD Operations Portal

ARC—Air Reserve Components

AV/HIPS – Anti-Virus/Host Intrusion Prevention System

BCQ—Basic Cyberspace Qualified

BMC—Basic Mission Capable

BPT—Be Prepared To

C2—Command & Control

CAP—Cyberspace Alert Patrol

CC—Commander

CCC—Crew Commander

CD—Deputy Commander; Compact Disk

CFT—Composite Force Training

CIP—Cyberspace Interdiction Package

CKP—Cyberspace Strike Package

COC—Operations Controller

CPI—Cybercrew Position Indicator

CSP—Cyberspace Surveillance Package

CT—Continuation Training

CV—Vice Commander

DCC – Defensive Counter-Cyberspace

DCO—Defensive cyberspace operations

DNS—Domain Name Server

DO—Director of Operations

DOC—Designed Operational Capability

DOK—Weapons and Tactics

DOT—Director of Operational Training

DVD—Digital Versatile Disk

EXP— Experienced

FLT—Flight

FTP—File Transfer Protocol

FTU—Formal Training Unit

HAF—Headquarters Air Force

HBS—Host Base Security

HBSS—Host Base Security System

HHQ—Higher Headquarters

HQ—Headquarters

IAW—In Accordance With

INEXP—Inexperienced

IQT—Initial Qualification Training

IRO—Incident Response

JFT—Joint Force Training

LFE—Large Force Exercise

LIMFAC—Limiting Factor

MAJCOM—Major Command

MC—Mission Commander

MISREP—Mission Report

MQT—Mission Qualification Training

MR/CMR—Mission Ready/Combat Mission Ready

N-BMC – Non-Basic Mission Capable

NGB—National Guard Bureau

NMR – Non-Mission Ready

OG—Operations Group

OPORD—Operations Order

OPR—Office of Primary Responsibility

OSS—Operations Support Squadron

PBED—Planning, Briefing, Execution, and Debriefing

PCAP—Packet Capture

PCS—Permanent Change of Station

QRF—Quick Reaction Force

RCP—Ready Cybercrew Program

RDS—Records Disposition Schedule

RM—Risk Management

ROC—Rehearsal of Concept

ROE—Rules of Engagement

RT—Requalification Training

RTM—RCP Tasking Memorandum

RTRB—Realistic Training Review Board

SORTS—Status of Resources and Training

SQ—Squadron

SSL—Secure Socket Layer

TDY—Temporary Duty

TRP—Tactical Reconnaissance Package

USAF—United States Air Force

USAFWS—United States Air Force Weapons School

USB—Universal Serial Bus

WIC—Weapons Instructor Course

Terms

Additional Training—Any training recommended to remedy deficiencies identified during an evaluation that must be completed by a specific due date. This training may include self-study, CTD, or simulator. Additional training must include demonstration of satisfactory knowledge or proficiency to examiner, supervisor or instructor (as stipulated in the Additional Training description) to qualify as completed.

Attached Personnel—This includes anyone not assigned to the unit but maintaining qualification through that unit. AFRC, ANG, and HAF augmented personnel are an example of attached personnel.

Basic Cyberspace Qualified (BCQ)—A crewmember who satisfactorily completed IQT. The crewmember will carry BCQ only until completion of MQT. BCQ crewmembers will not perform RCP-tasked events or sorties without instructor crewmembers.

Basic Mission Capable (BMC)—A crewmember who satisfactorily completed IQT and MQT, but is not in fully-certified MR/CMR status. The crewmember must be able to attain MR/CMR status to meet operational taskings as specified in the applicable instructional supplements. This status is primarily for individuals in units that perform weapon system-specific operational support functions (i.e., formal training units, operational test and tactics development). BMC requirements will be identified in the appropriate weapon system guidance.

Certification—Designation of an individual by the certifying official (normally the SQ/CC) as having completed required training and being capable of performing a specific duty.

Continuation Training (CT)— Training which provides crewmembers with the volume, frequency, and mix of training necessary to maintain currency and proficiency in the assigned qualification level.

Currency—A measure of how frequently and/or recently a task is completed. Currency requirements should ensure the average crewmember maintains a minimum level of proficiency in a specific event.

Cybercrew Position Indicator (CPI) – Codes used to manage crew positions to ensure a high state of readiness is maintained with available resources.—**Cyberspace Operations (CO)** – The employment of cyberspace capabilities where the primary purpose is to achieve objectives in or through cyberspace.

Experienced Crewmember (EXP)—Management term describing crewmembers who meet the requirement as dictated per within the weapon system specific volumes.

Initial Qualification Training (IQT)—Weapon system-specific training designed address system specific and/or positional specific training leading to declaration of BCQ as a prerequisite to Mission Qualification Training (MQT).

Instructor—An experienced individual qualified to instruct other individuals in mission area academics and positional duties. Instructors will be qualified appropriately to the level of the training they provide.

Instructor Event—An event logged by an instructor when performing instructor duties during the sortie, or a portion thereof. Instructor qualification required and used for the mission or a mission element. Examples include upgrade sorties, updating lost currencies, etc. Instructors will log this event on evaluation sorties.

Mission—A set of tasks that lead to an objective, to include associated planning, brief, execution, and debrief.

Mission Qualification Training (MQT)—Following IQT, MQT is a formal training program used to qualify crewmembers in assigned crew positions to perform the unit mission. This training is required to achieve a basic level of competence in unit's primary tasked missions and is a prerequisite for MR/CMR or BMC declaration.

Mission Ready/Combat Mission Ready (MR/CMR)—The status of a crewmember who satisfactorily completed IQT, MQT, and maintains certification, currency and proficiency in the command or unit operational mission.

One—Month Lookback – Total individual crewmember RCP sorties and events tracked over a preceding 30-day time period. This lookback is used to assess individual progress in achieving the total sorties and events (minimum) required for the 12-month training cycle.

Proficiency—A measure of how well a task is completed. A crewmember is considered proficient when they can perform tasks at the minimum acceptable levels of speed, accuracy, and safety.

Qualification (QUAL)—Designation of an individual by the unit commander as having completed required training and evaluation and being capable of performing a specific duty.

Ready Cybercrew Program (RCP)—Annual sortie/event training requirements for crewmembers to maintain mission ready/combat mission ready (MR/CMR) status.

Sortie—The actions an individual cyberspace weapon system takes to accomplish a mission and/or mission objective(s) within a defined start and stop period.

Special Mission Qualification—Training in any special skills (e.g., tactics, weapon system capabilities, responsibilities, etc.) necessary to perform the unit's assigned missions that are not required by every crewmember. Special Mission Qualification is normally accomplished after the crewmember is assigned MR/CMR or BMC status, and is normally in addition to MR/CMR or BMC requirements.

Squadron Supervisor—May include all or some of the following depending on specific guidance and SQ/CC concurrence: SQ/CC, SQ/DO, ADOs, and FLT/CCs.

Supervisory Crew or Staff Member—Personnel in supervisory or staff positions (CPI-6/8/B/D) who actively conduct cyberspace operations.

Supervised Status – The status of a crewmember who must perform missions/sorties under instructor supervision.—Three-Month Lookback – Total individual crewmember RCP sorties and events tracked over a preceding 90-day time period. This lookback is used to assess individual progress in achieving the total sorties and events (minimum) required for the 12-month training cycle.

Training Level—Assigned to individuals based on the continuation training status (basic cyberspace qualification, basic mission capable, or mission ready/combat mission ready) they are required to maintain.

Training Period—Any training period determined by the wing in which training requirements are performed.

Upgrade Training—Training needed to qualify to a crew position of additional responsibility for a specific weapon system.

Attachment 2

GLOSSARY OF MISSION, SORTIE AND EVENT DEFINITIONS

A2.1. Mission and Sortie Definitions:

A2.1.1. Commander Option Mission. Mission allocated by the unit commander to support individual training requirements and unit training objectives.

A2.1.2. Composite Force Training (CFT). Scenarios employing multiple units of the same or different weapon systems types, each under the direction of its own package leader, performing the same or different roles. Only one event may be logged per mission.

A2.1.3. Surveillance: Collect relevant data and information in/on the Area of Operations (AO).

A2.1.4. Reconnaissance: Collect relevant data and information on threats in the AO.

A2.1.5. Access: Provide sufficient access for supported cyber forces.

A2.1.6. Strike: Damage or destroy an objective or a capability.

A2.1.7. Escort: Provide support to cyber weapon system(s) conducting primary missions in assigned AO.

A2.1.8. Strike Coordination and Reconnaissance (SCAR): Conduct or facilitate dynamic targeting in the AO. Includes actions conducted under other tactical missions such as Surveillance, Reconnaissance and Strike.

A2.1.9. Secure: Enhance the defenses of the AO to mitigate risks.

A2.1.10. Threat Emulation: Replicate realistic TTP of specific cyber threats to evaluate cyber defenses and prepare DoD DCO.

A2.1.11. Joint Force Training (JFT). Scenarios employing integrated aerospace, land, naval, cyberspace forces to include other services. Only one event may be logged per mission.

A2.1.12. Mission Commander (MC) Mission. Special certification. Mission where crewmember acted as MC for a joint/composite mission responsible for two or more types of cyberspace weapon systems. May be logged in conjunction with other RCP mission requirements.

A2.2. Mission, Sortie and Event Identifiers and Descriptions:

Table A2.1. Identifiers.

Identifier	Group	Paragraph
GTR	Mission Related Training	A2.2.1
ACD	ACD Operator	A2.3.1
CCC	Crew Commander	A2.3.2
COC	Operations Controller	A2.3.3
DCC	Defensive Counter-Cyberspace	A2.3.4
HBS	Host-Base Security	A2.3.5
IRO	Incident Response	A2.3.6
XTR	Unit Defined Training	A2.3.7

A2.2.1. Mission-Related Training. Mission-related training is training required of all crewmembers as part of their CT program. Where conflict exists between this guidance and the RTM, the RTM takes precedence. Training accomplished during IQT/MQT may be credited toward CT requirements for the training cycle in which it was accomplished.

A2.2.1.1. GTR001 Unit Indoctrination Training.

A2.2.1.1.1. Purpose: Each newly assigned crewmember will complete a local unit indoctrination program prior to performing unsupervised primary crewmember duties. This is one-time training after a permanent change of station/assignment.

A2.2.1.1.2. Description: This training is required for all newly assigned and attached crewmembers. The unit will publish specific requirements. This training will prepare crewmembers for the unit's operational mission. The training will familiarize them with local procedures, facility/support agencies; introduce any unit/mission unique procedures, and other information as determined by the SQ/CC.

A2.2.1.1.3. OPR: Unit

A2.2.1.1.4. Course Developer: Unit

A2.2.1.1.5. Training Media: As required

A2.2.1.1.6. Additional Information: Document Unit Indoctrination Training in the individual's Training IQF for assigned and attached personnel.

A2.2.1.2. GTR002 Weapons and Tactics Training.

A2.2.1.2.1. Purpose: To provide the crewmember with the information necessary for effective and successful execution of the unit's assigned mission.

A2.2.1.2.2. Description: GTR002 will be administered using courseware developed by the unit. The course will be based on information found in AFTTP 3-1, AFTTP 3-3, AFI 17-2ACD V3 as well as other documents relevant to the execution of the unit's mission. Units will develop tests based on the documents listed in this paragraph and maintain a master question file. Test will be open book and consist of a minimum of 50 questions. To receive credit for this training each crewmember must complete an open book test with a minimum score of 80 percent.

A2.2.1.2.3. OPR: Unit/DOK

A2.2.1.2.4. Course Developer: Unit/DOK

A2.2.1.2.5. Training Media: Lecture & Test

A2.2.1.2.6. Instructor Requirements: Academic instructors should be WIC graduates or have attended the applicable academic portion(s) of school, if possible.

A2.2.1.2.7. Additional Information: Instructors teaching GTR002 may receive credit for their GTR002 requirement.

A2.2.1.3. GTR003 Risk Management (RM) Training.

A2.2.1.3.1. Purpose: To provide crewmembers with unit RM training according to AF Pamphlet 90-803, *Risk Management (RM) Guidelines and Tools*, other RM resources, and MAJCOM Supplements.

A2.2.1.3.2. Description: GTR003 will be administered using unit developed courseware. RM training introduces the common core RM subjects to provide crewmembers with the information necessary to enhance mission effectiveness. Training should create a cultural mindset in which every crewmember is trained and motivated to manage risk and integrates RM into mission and activity planning process ensures decisions are based upon risk assessment of the operation/activity. RM training will be tailored to meet the unique mission needs and operational requirements of each organization and to the personnel within the organization.

A2.2.1.3.3. OPR: Unit

A2.2.1.3.4. Course Developer: Unit

A2.2.1.3.5. Training Media: Lecture

A2.2.1.3.6. Additional Information: RM instructors teaching GTR003 may receive credit for their GTR003 requirement.

A2.3. Tactical Events. The following is a list of tactical events to be used for fulfilling tasked requirements.

A2.3.1. ACD Operator (ACD) CT Events.

A2.3.1.1. ACD001 Event Management

A2.3.1.1.1. Purpose: Learn/demonstrate event management procedures

A2.3.1.1.2. Description: Process an event from the standard alert aggregator and take necessary actions.

A2.3.1.1.3. OPR: Unit/DOT

A2.3.1.1.4. Course Developer: Unit/DOT

A2.3.1.1.5. Training Media: Lecture

A2.3.1.1.6. Instructor Requirements: Defender/ACD weapon System

A2.3.1.1.7. Additional Information: Student assessment via instructor observation; Course/Instructor feedback via questionnaire

A2.3.1.2. ACD002 Filter/Rule Management

A2.3.1.2.1. Purpose: Learn/demonstrate filter & rule management procedures

A2.3.1.2.2. Description: Create, modify, or remove alert filter and rules as required

A2.3.1.2.3. OPR: Unit/DOT

A2.3.1.2.4. Course Developer: Unit/DOT

A2.3.1.2.5. Training Media: Lecture

A2.3.1.2.6. Instructor Requirements: ArcSight, Defender/ACD weapon system

A2.3.1.2.7. Additional Information: Student assessment via instructor observation; Course/Instructor feedback via questionnaire

A2.3.1.3. ACD003 CAT 5 Processing

A2.3.1.3.1. Purpose: Learn/demonstrate understanding of CAT event processing

A2.3.1.3.2. Description: Perform any actions required to process a CAT 5 such as opening, reporting, closing, etc.

A2.3.1.3.3. OPR: Unit/DOT

A2.3.1.3.4. Course Developer: Unit/DOT

A2.3.1.3.5. Training Media: Lecture/Performance

A2.3.1.3.6. Instructor Requirements: Defender/Patriot, AOP & ACD weapon system

A2.3.1.3.7. Additional Information: Student assessment via instructor observation; Course/Instructor feedback via questionnaire

A2.3.1.4. ACD004 CAT 3/6 Processing

A2.3.1.4.1. Purpose: Learn/demonstrate understanding of CAT event processing

A2.3.1.4.2. Description: Perform any actions required to process a CAT 3/6 such as opening, reporting, closing, etc.

A2.3.1.4.3. OPR: Unit/DOT

A2.3.1.4.4. Course Developer: Unit/DOT

A2.3.1.4.5. Training Media: Lecture/Performance

A2.3.1.4.6. Instructor Requirements: Defender/Patriot, AOP & ACD weapon system

A2.3.1.4.7. Additional Information: Student assessment via instructor observation; Course/Instructor feedback via questionnaire

A2.3.1.5. ACD005 CAT 8 Processing

A2.3.1.5.1. Purpose: Learn/demonstrate understanding of CAT event processing

A2.3.1.5.2. Description: Perform any actions required to process a CAT 8 such as opening, reporting, closing, etc.

A2.3.1.5.3. OPR: Unit/DOT

A2.3.1.5.4. Course Developer: Unit/DOT

A2.3.1.5.5. Training Media: Lecture/Performance

A2.3.1.5.6. Instructor Requirements: Defender/Patriot, AOP & ACD weapon system

A2.3.1.5.7. Additional Information: Student assessment via instructor observation; Course/Instructor feedback via questionnaire

A2.3.1.6. ACD006 Historical Correlation/Research

A2.3.1.6.1. Purpose: Learn/demonstrate ability to correlate historical data and current events

A2.3.1.6.2. Description: Utilize historical analysis tools and capabilities to correlate current activity with prior activity.

A2.3.1.6.3. OPR: Unit/DOT

A2.3.1.6.4. Course Developer: Unit/DOT

A2.3.1.6.5. Training Media: Lecture/Performance

A2.3.1.6.6. Instructor Requirements: Defender/Patriot, AOP & ACD weapon system

A2.3.1.6.7. Additional Information: Student assessment via instructor observation; Course/Instructor feedback via questionnaire

A2.3.1.7. ACD007 Packet Capture (PCAP) Analysis

A2.3.1.7.1. Purpose: Conduct PCAP analysis to determine traffic direction and further investigate an event

A2.3.1.7.2. Description: Analyze PCAP data to identify and extract important supporting information for an event.

A2.3.1.7.3. OPR: Unit/DOT

A2.3.1.7.4. Course Developer: Unit/DOT

A2.3.1.7.5. Training Media. Lecture/Performance

A2.3.1.7.6. Instructor Requirements: Defender/Patriot, AOP & ACD weapon system

A2.3.1.7.7. Additional Information: Student assessment via instructor observation; Course/Instructor feedback via questionnaire

A2.3.1.8. ACD008 Research Alert Signature

A2.3.1.8.1. Purpose: Research a particular signature that fired on a specific event

A2.3.1.8.2. Description: Utilize available resources to determine what caused a specified alert to trigger.

A2.3.1.8.3. OPR: Unit/DOT

A2.3.1.8.4. Course Developer: Unit/DOT

A2.3.1.8.5. Training Media: Lecture/Performance

A2.3.1.8.6. Instructor Requirements: Defender/Patriot, AOP & ACD weapon system

A2.3.1.8.7. Additional Information: Student assessment via instructor observation; Course/Instructor feedback via questionnaire

A2.3.1.9. ACD009 Traffic Validation

A2.3.1.9.1. Purpose: Validate traffic

A2.3.1.9.2. Description: Utilize available resources to validate any traffic that cannot be confirmed as malicious or normal.

A2.3.1.9.3. OPR: Unit/DOT

A2.3.1.9.4. Course Developer: Unit/DOT

A2.3.1.9.5. Training Media: Lecture/Performance

A2.3.1.9.6. Instructor Requirements: Defender/Patriot, AOP & ACD weapon system

A2.3.1.9.7. Additional Information: Student assessment via instructor observation; Course/Instructor feedback via questionnaire

A2.3.2. Crew Commander (CCC) Training Events.

A2.3.2.1. CCC001 DCO Task Assignment

A2.3.2.1.1. Purpose: Practice C2 via Defense Connect Online chat between ACD unit and the Operations Center

A2.3.2.1.2. Description: Assign prioritized missions to available DCO forces.

A2.3.2.1.3. OPR: Unit/DOT

A2.3.2.1.4. Course Developer: Unit/DOT

A2.3.2.1.5. Training Media: Lecture/Performance

A2.3.2.1.6. Instructor Requirements: Defender/Patriot, AOP & ACD weapon system

A2.3.2.1.7. Additional Information: Student assessment via instructor observation; Course/Instructor feedback via questionnaire

A2.3.2.2. CCC002 Mission Command & Control (C2)

A2.3.2.2.1. Purpose: Practice C2 via Defense Connect Online chat between ACD unit and the Operations Center

A2.3.2.2.2. Description: Use standard C2 channels to coordinate mission with participating partners.

A2.3.2.2.3. OPR: Unit/DOT

A2.3.2.2.4. Course Developer: Unit/DOT

A2.3.2.2.5. Training Media: Lecture/Performance

A2.3.2.2.6. Instructor Requirements: Defender/Patriot, AOP & ACD weapon system

A2.3.2.2.7. Additional Information: Student assessment via instructor observation; Course/Instructor feedback via questionnaire

A2.3.2.3. CCC003 Mission Emergency Procedures

A2.3.2.3.1. Purpose: Demonstrate ability to successfully run emergency action plan/procedures

A2.3.2.3.2. Description: Perform emergency procedures for any issue affecting mission completion.

A2.3.2.3.3. OPR: Unit/DOT

A2.3.2.3.4. Course Developer: Unit/DOT

A2.3.2.3.5. Training Media: Lecture/Performance

A2.3.2.3.6. Instructor Requirements: Defender/Patriot, AOP & ACD weapon system

A2.3.2.3.7. Additional Information: Student assessment via instructor observation; Course/Instructor feedback via questionnaire

A2.3.2.4. CCC004 Quick Reaction Force Employment

A2.3.2.4.1. Purpose: Receive a tasking from the Operations Center to activate a QRF; task or re-task forces as available

A2.3.2.4.2. Description: Reprioritize forces and assign quick reaction tasks to the necessary forces.

A2.3.2.4.3. OPR: Unit/DOT

A2.3.2.4.4. Course Developer: Unit/DOT

A2.3.2.4.5. Training Media: Lecture

A2.3.2.4.6. Instructor Requirements: Defender/Patriot, AOP & ACD weapon system

A2.3.2.4.7. Additional Information: Student assessment via instructor observation; Course/Instructor feedback via questionnaire

A2.3.3. Operations Controller (COC) Training Events.

A2.3.3.1. COC001 DCO Task Assignment

A2.3.3.1.1. Purpose: Practice C2 via Defense Connect Online chat between ACD unit and the Operations Center

A2.3.3.1.2. Description: Assign prioritized tasks to available DCO forces.

A2.3.3.1.3. OPR: Unit/DOT

A2.3.3.1.4. Course Developer: Unit/DOT

A2.3.3.1.5. Training Media: Lecture

A2.3.3.1.6. Instructor Requirements: Defender/Patriot, AOP & ACD weapon system

A2.3.3.1.7. Additional Information: Student assessment via instructor observation; Course/Instructor feedback via questionnaire

A2.3.3.2. COC002 Mission Command & Control

A2.3.3.2.1. Purpose: Practice C2 via Defense Connect Online chat between ACD unit and the Operations Center

A2.3.3.2.2. Description: Use standard C2 channels to coordinate mission with participating partners.

A2.3.3.2.3. OPR: Unit/DOT

A2.3.3.2.4. Course Developer: Unit/DOT

A2.3.3.2.5. Training Media: Lecture

A2.3.3.2.6. Instructor Requirements: Defender/Patriot, AOP & ACD weapon system

A2.3.3.2.7. Additional Information: Student assessment via instructor observation; Course/Instructor feedback via questionnaire

A2.3.3.3. COC003 Mission Emergency Procedures

A2.3.3.3.1. Purpose: Demonstrate ability to successfully run emergency action plan/procedures

A2.3.3.3.2. Description: Perform emergency procedures for any issue affecting mission completion.

A2.3.3.3.3. OPR: Unit/DOT

A2.3.3.3.4. Course Developer: Unit/DOT

A2.3.3.3.5. Training Media: Lecture

A2.3.3.3.6. Instructor Requirements: Checklists, EAP & AOP

A2.3.3.3.7. Additional Information: Student assessment via instructor observation; Course/Instructor feedback via questionnaire

A2.3.3.4. COC004 Quick Reaction Force Employment

A2.3.3.4.1. Purpose: Receive a tasking from the Operations Center to activate a QRF; task or re-task forces as available

A2.3.3.4.2. Description: Reprioritize forces and assign quick reaction tasks to the necessary forces.

A2.3.3.4.3. OPR: Unit/DOT

A2.3.3.4.4. Course Developer: Unit/DOT

A2.3.3.4.5. Training Media: Lecture

A2.3.3.4.6. Instructor Requirements: Defender/Patriot, AOP & ACD weapon system

A2.3.3.4.7. Additional Information: Student assessment via instructor observation; Course/Instructor feedback via questionnaire

A2.3.4. ACD Operator - Defensive Counter-Cyberspace (DCC) Training Events.

A2.3.4.1. DCC001 Wide Scope Survey

A2.3.4.1.1. Purpose: Conduct DCC Operations

A2.3.4.1.2. Description: Deploy survey tools via mission system to all specified terrain/assets.

A2.3.4.1.3. OPR: Unit/DOT

A2.3.4.1.4. Course Developer: Unit/DOT

A2.3.4.1.5. Training Media: Lecture/Performance

A2.3.4.1.6. Instructor Requirements: Defender/Patriot, AOP & ACD weapon system

A2.3.4.1.7. Additional Information: Student assessment via instructor observation; Course/Instructor feedback via questionnaire

A2.3.4.2. DCC002 Remote System Analysis (via Standalone)

A2.3.4.2.1. Purpose: Conduct DCC Operations

A2.3.4.2.2. Description: Utilize a standalone remote forensics or analysis tool to analyze specified terrain.

A2.3.4.2.3. OPR: Unit/DOT

A2.3.4.2.4. Course Developer: Unit/DOT

A2.3.4.2.5. Training Media: Lecture/Performance

A2.3.4.2.6. Instructor Requirements: Defender/Patriot, AOP & ACD weapon system

A2.3.4.2.7. Additional Information: Student assessment via instructor observation; Course/Instructor feedback via questionnaire

A2.3.4.3. DCC003 Remote System Analysis (via Operating System [OS])

A2.3.4.3.1. Purpose: Conduct DCC Operations

A2.3.4.3.2. Description: Utilize tools built-in or added on to a Windows or UNIX platform to perform remote analysis of a specified terrain.

A2.3.4.3.3. OPR: Unit/DOT

A2.3.4.3.4. Course Developer: Unit/DOT

A2.3.4.3.5. Training Media: Lecture/Performance

A2.3.4.3.6. Instructor Requirements: (AF Network access)/Defender/Patriot, AOP & ACD weapon system

A2.3.4.3.7. Additional Information: Student assessment via instructor observation; Course/Instructor feedback via questionnaire

A2.3.4.4. DCC004 Capability Maintenance

A2.3.4.4.1. Purpose: Conduct DCC Operations

A2.3.4.4.2. Description: Modify a capability to correct errors or improve efficiency.

A2.3.4.4.3. OPR: Unit/DOT

A2.3.4.4.4. Course Developer: Unit/DOT

A2.3.4.4.5. Training Media: Lecture/Performance

A2.3.4.4.6. Instructor Requirements: (AF Network access)/Defender/Patriot, AOP & ACD weapon system

A2.3.4.4.7. Additional Information: Student assessment via instructor observation; Course/Instructor feedback via questionnaire

A2.3.4.5. DCC005 Individual Host Deep-Dive

A2.3.4.5.1. Purpose: Conduct DCC Operations

A2.3.4.5.2. Description: Establish a session with the specified system to retrieve current data identified as having suspicious properties based on previous scans or intelligence reports.

A2.3.4.5.3. OPR: Unit/DOT

A2.3.4.5.4. Course Developer: Unit/DOT

A2.3.4.5.5. Training Media: Lecture/Performance

A2.3.4.5.6. Instructor Requirements: (AF Network access)/Defender/Patriot, AOP & ACD weapon system

A2.3.4.5.7. Additional Information: Student assessment via instructor observation; Course/Instructor feedback via questionnaire

A2.3.4.6. DCC006 Kill Active Connections

A2.3.4.6.1. Purpose: Conduct DCC Operations

A2.3.4.6.2. Description: Terminate connections via approved methods on a specified terrain.

A2.3.4.6.3. OPR: Unit/DOT

A2.3.4.6.4. Course Developer: Unit/DOT

A2.3.4.6.5. Training Media: Lecture/Performance

A2.3.4.6.6. Instructor Requirements: (AF Network access)/Defender/Patriot, AOP & ACD weapon system

A2.3.4.6.7. Additional Information: Student assessment via instructor observation; Course/Instructor feedback via questionnaire

A2.3.4.7. DCC007 Kill Active Processes

A2.3.4.7.1. Purpose: Conduct DCC Operations

A2.3.4.7.2. Description: Terminate processes via approved methods on a specified terrain.

A2.3.4.7.3. OPR: Unit/DOT

A2.3.4.7.4. Course Developer: Unit/DOT

A2.3.4.7.5. Training Media: Lecture/Performance

A2.3.4.7.6. Instructor Requirements: (AF Network access)/Defender/Patriot, AOP & ACD weapon system

A2.3.4.7.7. Additional Information: Student assessment via instructor observation; Course/Instructor feedback via questionnaire

A2.3.4.8. DCC008 Reporting

A2.3.4.8.1. Purpose: Close out mission activities via MISREP to ensure the Operations Center is aware of actions taken

A2.3.4.8.2. Description: Complete MISREP using standard medium once sortie is complete.

A2.3.4.8.3. OPR: Unit/DOT

A2.3.4.8.4. Course Developer: Unit/DOT

A2.3.4.8.5. Training Media: Lecture/Performance

A2.3.4.8.6. Instructor Requirements: Defender/Patriot, AOP & ACD weapon system

A2.3.4.8.7. Additional Information: Student assessment via instructor observation; Course/Instructor feedback via questionnaire

A2.3.5. ACD Operator – Host-Base Security (HBS) Training Events.

A2.3.5.1. HBS001 Host Alert Query

A2.3.5.1.1. Purpose: Conduct HBSS Operations

A2.3.5.1.2. Description: Run standard queries on alert aggregator.

A2.3.5.1.3. OPR: Unit/DOT

A2.3.5.1.4. Course Developer: Unit/DOT

A2.3.5.1.5. Training Media: Lecture/Hands on

A2.3.5.1.6. Instructor Requirements: (AF Network access)/Defender/Patriot, AOP & ACD weapon system

A2.3.5.1.7. Additional Information: Student assessment via instructor observation; Course/Instructor feedback via questionnaire

A2.3.5.2. HBS002 Process Query Results

A2.3.5.2.1. Purpose: Conduct HBS Operations

A2.3.5.2.2. Description: Perform required actions for any suspect results.

A2.3.5.2.3. OPR: Unit/DOT

A2.3.5.2.4. Course Developer: Unit/DOT

A2.3.5.2.5. Training Media: Lecture/Hands on

A2.3.5.2.6. Instructor Requirements: (AF Network access)/Defender/Patriot, AOP & ACD weapon system

A2.3.5.2.7. Additional Information: Student assessment via instructor observation; Course/Instructor feedback via questionnaire

A2.3.5.3. HBS003 Reporting

A2.3.5.3.1. Purpose: Close out mission activities via MISREP to ensure the Operations Center is aware of actions taken

A2.3.5.3.2. Description: Report any findings via standard reporting process.

A2.3.5.3.3. OPR: Unit/DOT

A2.3.5.3.4. Course Developer: Unit/DOT

A2.3.5.3.5. Training Media: Lecture/Hands on

A2.3.5.3.6. Instructor Requirements: Defender/Patriot, AOP & ACD weapon system

A2.3.5.3.7. Additional Information: Student assessment via instructor observation; Course/Instructor feedback via questionnaire

A2.3.6. ACD Operator - Incident Response (IRO) Training Events.

A2.3.6.1. IRO001 Data Research

A2.3.6.1.1. Purpose: Conduct Incident Response Activities

A2.3.6.1.2. Description: Utilize available resources (NIPR, SIPR, etc.) to research suspicious activity.

A2.3.6.1.3. OPR: Unit/DOT

A2.3.6.1.4. Course Developer: Unit/DOT

A2.3.6.1.5. Training Media: Lecture/Hands on

A2.3.6.1.6. Instructor Requirements: (AF Network access)/Defender/Patriot, AOP & ACD weapon system

A2.3.6.1.7. Additional Information: Student assessment via instructor observation; Course/Instructor feedback via questionnaire

A2.3.6.2. IRO002 DNS Log Analysis

A2.3.6.2.1. Purpose: Conduct Incident Response Activities

A2.3.6.2.2. Description: Review and suspicious activity from DNS logs for specified system(s).

A2.3.6.2.3. OPR: Unit/DOT

A2.3.6.2.4. Course Developer: Unit/DOT

A2.3.6.2.5. Training Media: Lecture/Hands on

A2.3.6.2.6. Instructor Requirements: (AF Network access)/Defender/Patriot, AOP & ACD weapon system

A2.3.6.2.7. Additional Information: Student assessment via instructor observation; Course/Instructor feedback via questionnaire

A2.3.6.3. IRO003 Event Closing

A2.3.6.3.1. Purpose: Conduct Incident Response Activities

A2.3.6.3.2. Description: Take the required steps to close an event.

A2.3.6.3.3. OPR: Unit/DOT

A2.3.6.3.4. Course Developer: Unit/DOT

A2.3.6.3.5. Training Media: Lecture/Hands on

A2.3.6.3.6. Instructor Requirements: (AF Network access)/Defender/Patriot, AOP & ACD weapon system

A2.3.6.3.7. Additional Information: Student assessment via instructor observation; Course/Instructor feedback via questionnaire

A2.3.6.4. IRO004 Event Opening

A2.3.6.4.1. Purpose: Conduct Incident Response Activities

A2.3.6.4.2. Description: Take the required steps to open an event based on suspicious activity.

A2.3.6.4.3. OPR: Unit/DOT

A2.3.6.4.4. Course Developer: Unit/DOT

A2.3.6.4.5. Training Media: Lecture/Hands on

A2.3.6.4.6. Instructor Requirements: (AF Network access)/Defender/Patriot, AOP & ACD weapon system

A2.3.6.4.7. Additional Information: Student assessment via instructor observation; Course/Instructor feedback via questionnaire

A2.3.6.5. IRO005 Incident Upgrade

A2.3.6.5.1. Purpose: Conduct Incident Response Activities

A2.3.6.5.2. Description: Lead or assist in upgrading an event to an incident.

A2.3.6.5.3. OPR: Unit/DOT

A2.3.6.5.4. Course Developer: Unit/DOT

A2.3.6.5.5. Training Media: Lecture

A2.3.6.5.6. Instructor Requirements: Defender/Patriot, AOP & ACD weapon system

A2.3.6.5.7. Additional Information: Student assessment via instructor observation; Course/Instructor feedback via questionnaire

A2.3.6.6. IRO006 Internet History Analysis

A2.3.6.6.1. Purpose: Conduct Incident Response Activities

A2.3.6.6.2. Description: Review routine and suspicious network activity from internet history for specified system(s).

A2.3.6.6.3. OPR: Unit/DOT

A2.3.6.6.4. Course Developer: Unit/DOT

A2.3.6.6.5. Training Media: Lecture/Performance

A2.3.6.6.6. Instructor Requirements: Defender/Patriot, AOP & ACD weapon system

A2.3.6.6.7. Additional Information: Student assessment via instructor observation; Course/Instructor feedback via questionnaire

A2.3.6.7. IRO007 Network Firewall Log Analysis

A2.3.6.7.1. Purpose: Conduct Incident Response Activities

A2.3.6.7.2. Description: Review routine and suspicious network activity from network firewall logs for specified system(s).

A2.3.6.7.3. OPR: Unit/DOT

A2.3.6.7.4. Course Developer: Unit/DOT

A2.3.6.7.5. Training Media: Lecture/Performance

A2.3.6.7.6. Instructor Requirements: Defender/Patriot, AOP & ACD weapon system

A2.3.6.7.7. Additional Information: Student assessment via instructor observation; Course/Instructor feedback via questionnaire

A2.3.6.8. IRO008 PCAP Analysis

A2.3.6.8.1. Purpose: Conduct PCAP analysis to determine traffic direction and further investigate an event

A2.3.6.8.2. Description: Review routine and suspicious network activity from PCAP data for specified system(s).

A2.3.6.8.3. OPR: Unit/DOT

A2.3.6.8.4. Course Developer: Unit/DOT

A2.3.6.8.5. Training Media: Lecture/Performance

A2.3.6.8.6. Instructor Requirements: Defender/Patriot, AOP & ACD weapon system

A2.3.6.8.7. Additional Information: Student assessment via instructor observation; Course/Instructor feedback via questionnaire

A2.3.6.9. IRO009 Additional Data Processing

A2.3.6.9.1. Purpose: Conduct Incident Response Activities

A2.3.6.9.2. Description: Properly retrieve and store data received from external sources via Compact Disks (CDs), Digital Versatile Disks (DVDs), email, File Transfer Protocol (FTP), websites, etc.

A2.3.6.9.3. OPR: Unit/DOT

A2.3.6.9.4. Course Developer: Unit/DOT

A2.3.6.9.5. Training Media: Lecture/Performance

A2.3.6.9.6. Instructor Requirements: (AF Network access)/Defender/Patriot, AOP & ACD weapon system

A2.3.6.9.7. Additional Information: Student assessment via instructor observation; Course/Instructor feedback via questionnaire

A2.3.6.10. IRO010 Proxy Log Analysis

A2.3.6.10.1. Purpose: Conduct Incident Response Activities

A2.3.6.10.2. Description: Review routine and suspicious network activity from proxy logs for specified system(s).

A2.3.6.10.3. OPR: Unit/DOT

A2.3.6.10.4. Course Developer: Unit/DOT

A2.3.6.10.5. Training Media: Lecture/Performance

A2.3.6.10.6. Instructor Requirements: (AF Network access)/Defender/Patriot, AOP & ACD weapon system

A2.3.6.10.7. Additional Information: Student assessment via instructor observation; Course/Instructor feedback via questionnaire

A2.3.6.11. IRO011 Remote Artifact Retrieval

A2.3.6.11.1. Purpose: Conduct Incident Response Activities

A2.3.6.11.2. Description: Retrieve Anti-Virus/Host Intrusion Prevention System (AV/HIPS) logs, internet history, quarantined files, Universal Serial Bus (USB) history, or event logs from remote systems.

A2.3.6.11.3. OPR: Unit/DOT

A2.3.6.11.4. Course Developer: Unit/DOT

A2.3.6.11.5. Training Media: Lecture/Performance

A2.3.6.11.6. Instructor Requirements: Defender/Patriot, AOP & ACD weapon system

A2.3.6.11.7. Additional Information: Student assessment via instructor observation; Course/Instructor feedback via questionnaire

A2.3.6.12. IRO012 Router Log Analysis

A2.3.6.12.1. Purpose: Conduct Incident Response Activities

A2.3.6.12.2. Description: Review routine and suspicious network activity from router logs for specified system(s).

A2.3.6.12.3. OPR: Unit/DOT

A2.3.6.12.4. Course Developer: Unit/DOT

A2.3.6.12.5. Training Media: Lecture/Performance

A2.3.6.12.6. Instructor Requirements: Defender/Patriot, AOP & ACD weapon system

A2.3.6.12.7. Additional Information: Student assessment via instructor observation; Course/Instructor feedback via questionnaire

A2.3.6.13. IRO013 SSI Traffic Analysis

A2.3.6.13.1. Purpose: Conduct Incident Response Activities

A2.3.6.13.2. Description: Decrypt captured Secure Socket Layer (SSL) using private keys in Wireshark to suspicious traffic.

A2.3.6.13.3. OPR: Unit/DOT

A2.3.6.13.4. Course Developer: Unit/DOT

A2.3.6.13.5. Training Media: Lecture/Performance

A2.3.6.13.6. Instructor Requirements: Defender/Patriot, AOP & ACD weapon system

A2.3.6.13.7. Additional Information: Student assessment via instructor observation; Course/Instructor feedback via questionnaire

A2.3.6.14. IRO014 System Snapshot Analysis

A2.3.6.14.1. Purpose: Conduct Incident Response Activities

A2.3.6.14.2. Description: Review routine and suspicious network activity from system snapshot for specified system(s).

A2.3.6.14.3. OPR: Unit/DOT

A2.3.6.14.4. Course Developer: Unit/DOT

A2.3.6.14.5. Training Media: Lecture/Performance

A2.3.6.14.6. Instructor Requirements: Defender/Patriot, AOP & ACD weapon system

A2.3.6.14.7. Additional Information: Student assessment via instructor observation; Course/Instructor feedback via questionnaire

A2.3.6.15. IRO015 USB History Analysis

A2.3.6.15.1. Purpose: Conduct Incident Response Activities

A2.3.6.15.2. Description: Review routine and suspicious activity from USB removable devices history for specified system(s).

A2.3.6.15.3. OPR: Unit/DOT

A2.3.6.15.4. Course Developer: Unit/DOT

A2.3.6.15.5. Training Media: Lecture/Performance

A2.3.6.15.6. Instructor Requirements: Defender/Patriot, AOP & ACD weapon system

A2.3.6.15.7. Additional Information: Student assessment via instructor observation; Course/Instructor feedback via questionnaire

A2.3.6.16. IRO016 Web Server Log Analysis

A2.3.6.16.1. Purpose: Conduct Incident Response Activities

A2.3.6.16.2. Description: Review routine and suspicious network activity from web server logs for specified system(s).

A2.3.6.16.3. OPR: Unit/DOT

A2.3.6.16.4. Course Developer: Unit/DOT

A2.3.6.16.5. Training Media: Lecture/Performance

A2.3.6.16.6. Instructor Requirements: Defender/Patriot, AOP & ACD weapon system

A2.3.6.16.7. Additional Information: Student assessment via instructor observation; Course/Instructor feedback via questionnaire

A2.3.6.17. IRO017 Windows Event Log Analysis

A2.3.6.17.1. Purpose: Conduct Incident Response Activities

A2.3.6.17.2. Description: Review routine and suspicious activity from Windows event logs for specified system(s).

A2.3.6.17.3. OPR: Unit/DOT

A2.3.6.17.4. Course Developer: Unit/DOT

A2.3.6.17.5. Training Media: Lecture/Performance

A2.3.6.17.6. Instructor Requirements: Defender/Patriot, AOP & ACD weapon system

A2.3.6.17.7. Additional Information: Student assessment via instructor observation; Course/Instructor feedback via questionnaire

A2.3.7. Unit Defined ("XTR") Training Requirements. XTR is reserved for use by local units. Publish OG/CC level guidance documenting local event identifiers, associated nomenclature, volume, currency and frequency. OG/CC should review all "XTR" training requirements for relevancy to the unit's mission.

Attachment 3

CERTIFICATION GUIDE

A3.1. Outlines for Briefs. The following outline is a guide for the development of certification briefs:

A3.1.1. Overview:

A3.1.2. Introduction (participants and brief classification)

A3.1.3. Status of friendly forces:

A3.1.4. Area of Operations:

A3.1.5. Status of Enemy Forces:

A3.1.6. Mission Employment Brief:

A3.1.7. Essential Elements of Information/Reports:

Attachment 4

CREWMEMBER RESOURCE MANAGEMENT

A4.1. Crew inventory requires close management at all levels to ensure a high state of readiness is maintained with available resources.   To manage crewmember inventory, Crewmember Position Indicator (CPI) codes are assigned to identify these positions.

Table A4.1. Cybercrew Position Indicator (CPI) Codes.

CPI Codes	Explanation	Remarks
1	Crewmember position used primarily for weapon system operations (Officer).	See Note 1
2	Crewmember position used primarily for weapon system operations (Government Civilians).	See Note 1
3	Staff or supervisory positions at wing level and below that have responsibilities and duties that require cyberspace operations expertise but which do not require the incumbents to operate the weapon system.	See Note 2
4	Staff or supervisory positions above the wing level that have responsibilities and duties that require cyberspace operations expertise but which do not require the incumbents to operate the weapon system.	See Note 2
6	Staff or supervisory positions at wing level and below that have responsibilities and duties that require the incumbents to actively perform cyberspace operational duties on the weapon system.	See Note 2
8	Staff or supervisory positions above the wing level that have responsibilities and duties that require the incumbent to actively conduct cyberspace operations on the weapon system.	See Note 2
A	Crew positions used primarily for weapon system operations (Enlisted).	See Note 1
B	Staff or supervisory positions at wing level and below that have responsibilities and duties that require the incumbents to actively perform cyberspace operational duties on the weapon system.	See Note 2
C	Staff or supervisory positions at wing level and below that have responsibilities and duties that require cyberspace operations expertise but which do not require the incumbents to actively operate the weapon system.	See Note 2
D	Staff or supervisory positions above the wing level that have responsibilities and duties that require the incumbent to actively conduct cyberspace operations on a weapon system.	See Note 2
E	Staff or supervisory positions above the wing level that have responsibilities and duties that require cyberspace operations expertise but which do not require the incumbents to actively	See Note 2

	operate the weapon system.	
Z	Crew positions used primarily for weapon system operations (Contractor).	See Note 1

Notes:
1. CPI-1, 2, A and Z are for officers, enlisted, government civilian, and contractor personnel assigned to operational squadrons or formal training programs. The primary duty of these personnel is to operate the weapon system to conduct cyberspace operations.
2. CPI-3, 4, 6, 8, B, C, D, and E identify cyber crewmembers assigned to supervisory or staff positions. These positions require cyberspace operations experience with some requiring weapon system operation (CPI-6, 8, B, and D).

BY ORDER OF THE SECRETARY
OF THE AIR FORCE

AIR FORCE INSTRUCTION 17-2ACD
VOLUME 2

27 APRIL 2017

Cyberspace

AIR FORCE CYBERSPACE DEFENSE
(ACD) STANDARDIZATION AND
EVALUATION

COMPLIANCE WITH THIS PUBLICATION IS MANDATORY

ACCESSIBILITY: Publications and forms are available on the Publishing website at www.e-Publishing.af.mil for downloading or ordering

RELEASABILITY: There are no releasability restrictions on this publication

OPR: HQ USAF/A3CX/A6CX

Certified by: HQ USAF/A3C/A6C
(Brig Gen Kevin B. Kennedy)
Pages: 32

This Instruction implements Air Force (AF) Policy Directive (AFPD) 17-2, *Cyberspace Operations* and references Air Force Instruction (AFI) 17-202V2, *Cybercrew Standardization and Evaluation Program*. It establishes the Crew Standardization and Evaluation (Stan/Eval) procedures and evaluation criteria for qualifying crew members in the Air Force Cyber Defense (ACD) weapon system. This publication applies to all military and civilian AF personnel, members of AF Reserve Command (AFRC) units and the Air National Guard (ANG). Refer to paragraph 1.3 for information on the authority to waive provisions of this AFI. This publication may be supplemented at the unit level, but all direct supplements must be routed through channels to HQ USAF/A3C/A6C for coordination prior to certification and approval. The authorities to waive wing/unit level requirements in this publication are identified with a Tier ("T-0, T-1, T-2, T-3") number following the compliance statement. See AFI 33-360, *Publications and Forms Management*, Table 1.1, for a description of the authorities associated with the Tier numbers. Submit requests for waivers through the chain of command to the appropriate Tier waiver approval authority, or alternately, to the Publication OPR for non-tiered compliance items. Send recommended changes or comments to the Office of Primary Responsibility (OPR) (HQ USAF/A3C/A6C, 1480 Air Force Pentagon, Washington, DC 20330-1480), using AF Form 847, *Recommendation for Change of Publication*; route AF Forms 847 from the field through the chain of command. This Instruction requires collecting and maintaining information protected by the Privacy Act of 1974 (5 U.S.C. 552a). System of records notices F036 AF PC C, Military Personnel Records System, and OPM/GOVT-1, General Personnel Records, apply. When collecting and maintaining information protect it by the Privacy

Act of 1974 authorized by 10 U.S.C. 8013. Ensure all records created as a result of processes prescribed in this publication are maintained in accordance with (IAW) AF Manual (AFMAN) 33-363, *Management of Records*, and disposed of in accordance with the AF Records Disposition Schedule (RDS) located in the AF Records Management Information System (AFRIMS). See Attachment 1 for a glossary of references and supporting information.

Chapter 1

GENERAL INFORMATION

1.1. General. This instruction provides cyberspace operations examiners and crew members with procedures and evaluation criteria used during performance evaluations on operational cyberspace weapon systems. For evaluation purposes, refer to this AFI for evaluation standards. Adherence to these procedures and criteria will ensure an accurate assessment of the proficiency and capabilities of crew members. In addition to general criteria information and grading criteria, this AFI provides specific information and grading criteria for each crew position, special mission qualification (SMQ), instructor upgrade qualification, and stan/eval examiner (SEE) objectivity evaluations.

1.2. Recommending Changes. Submit recommendations for improvements to this Instruction on AF Form 847 through the chain of command to HQ USAF/A3CX/A6CX. Approved recommendations will be collated into interim or formal change notices, and forwarded to HQ 24 AF/A3T for HQ 24 AF/A3 approval.

1.3. Waivers. Unless another approval authority is cited ("T-0, T-1, T-2, T-3"), waiver authority for this volume is the MAJCOM/A3 (or equivalent). Submit requests for waivers using AF FM 679 through the chain of command to the appropriate Tier waiver approval authority. If approved, waivers remain in effect for the life of the published guidance, unless the waiver authority specifies a shorter period of time, cancels in writing, or issues a change that alters the basis for the waiver.

1.4. Standardization and Evaluation Examiners (SEEs) will use the grading policies contained in AFI 17-202V2 and the evaluation criteria in this Instruction for conducting all weapon system performance, Crew Training Device (CTD), and Emergency Procedures Evaluations (EPE).

1.4.1. All evaluations assume a stable platform and normal operating conditions. Compound emergency procedures (more than one simultaneous emergency procedure) will not be used. **(T-2)**

1.4.2. Each squadron will design and maintain evaluation profiles for each mission/weapon system that includes information on each crew position. These profiles, approved by the Operations Group Stan/Eval office (OGV), should outline the minimum number and type of events to be performed/observed in order to satisfy a complete evaluation. Evaluation profiles will incorporate requirements set in the applicable grading criteria and reflect the primary unit tasking. **(T-3)**

1.4.3. All evaluations fall under the Qualification (QUAL), Mission (MSN) or Spot (SPOT) categories listed in AFI 17-202V2. For dual/multiple qualification or difference evaluations (an evaluation that covers major changes in an existing capability, e.g. a major upgrade to sensor suite adding that adds or alters capabilities) that do not update an eligibility period, list as "SPOT" on the front of the AF Form 4418, *Certificate of Cybercrew Qualification*, and explain that it was a difference evaluation under "Mission Description." **(T-2)**

1.4.3.1. Schedule all evaluation activity on one mission/sortie to the greatest extent possible. All performance phase requirements should be accomplished during a training (or operational if training not available) mission/sortie. If a required event is not accomplished during a mission/sortie, Operations Group commander (OG/CC) is the waiver authority for the event to be completed in the CTD. This may be delegated no lower than the Squadron commander (SQ/CC) unless otherwise authorized in position specific chapters of this Instruction. **(T-3)**

1.4.3.2. During all evaluations, any grading areas observed by the evaluator may be evaluated. If additional training is required for areas outside of the scheduled evaluation, document the training required under the appropriate area on the AF Form 4418. **(T-3)**

1.4.3.3. This Instruction contains a table of requirements for the written requisites and a table for the grading criteria for various evaluations. Each table may include a "Note" which refers to a general note found in the individual grading criteria, and/or a number which refers to a note shown below the table. To complete an evaluation, all areas annotated with an "R" must be successfully completed. **(T-3)**

1.4.3.4. Unit examiners may give evaluations outside of their organization to include administering evaluations between AFSPC, AFRC and ANG provided written agreements/understandings between the affected organizations are in-place. Written agreements/understandings shall be reviewed and updated annually. **(T-3)**

1.4.4. Momentary deviations from tolerances will not be considered in the grading, provided the examinee applies prompt corrective action and such deviations do not jeopardize safety or the mission. Cumulative deviations will be considered when determining the overall grade. The SEE will state the examinee's overall rating, review with the examinee the area grades assigned, thoroughly critique specific deviations, and recommend/assign any required additional training. **(T-2)**

1.4.5. SEEs will not evaluate students with whom they have instructed more than 50% of the qualification/upgrade training performance events without SQ/CC approval. SEEs will not evaluate students they recommended for end of training qualification/upgrade evaluation unless approved by the SQ/CC. **(T-3)**

1.4.6. All crewmembers for the mission/sortie (to include students, instructors, examinees, and evaluators) will participate in and adhere to all required mission planning, mission briefing, mission execution, and mission debriefing requirements. All crewmembers must be current on Crewmember Information Folders (CIF) and meet all Go/No-Go requirements IAW 17-202 series instructions, this Instruction, and all applicable supplemental guidance prior to operating, instructing, or evaluating on the weapon system. **(T-2)**

1.5. General Evaluation Requirements

1.5.1. Publications Check. In units where crewmembers are individually issued operating manuals, checklists, crew aids, etc., for use in conducting operations, a publications check will be accomplished for all evaluations. The publications check will be annotated in the Comments block of the AF Form 4418 only if unsatisfactory. List of Effective Pages (LEP) and annual "A" page checks in individually issued operating manuals must be accomplished, documented, and current. OGV will list the required operating publications each crew member is responsible for in the local CIF Library and/or local supplement to AFI 17-202V2.

NOTE: In units where such resources are not individually issued but made available/accessible for common use, the unit Stan/Eval office will list those items (version and date) and ensure the accuracy and currency of the information contained in those resources for common use. **(T-2)**

1.5.2. Written Examinations.

1.5.2.1. The requisites in Table 1.1 are common to all ACD crew positions and will be accomplished IAW AFI 17-202V2, all applicable supplemental guidance, and unit directives. These will be accomplished prior to the mission/sortie performance phase unless in conjunction with a No-Notice (N/N) QUAL. NOTE: A N/N evaluation conducted in the examinee's eligibility period and meeting all required QUAL profile requirements allows the examinee to opt for the N/N evaluation to satisfy a periodic QUAL, in which the examinee may complete written and Emergency Procedures Evaluation (EPE) requisites after the performance phase. However, the written examination(s) and EPE must be completed prior to the examinee's expiration date. **(T-2)**

1.5.3. EPE. Every Qualification evaluation which updates an expiration date will include an EPE. Qualification EPEs will evaluate the crewmember's knowledge and/or performance of emergency procedures, to include use of emergency equipment. Use the Emergency Procedures/Equipment grading criteria for all emergency situations given. Use Systems Knowledge/Operations grading criteria to evaluate general systems operation. An EPE will be accomplished orally and may be accomplished prior to the mission with any unit SEE conducting a scenario-based evaluation using question/answer (Q&A) techniques, preferably during the SEE pre-brief with the examinee. Units will determine scenarios for EPEs. The SEE will assign an overall EPE grade (1 or 3). Document the accomplishment and result of the EPE in the Written Phase block of Section II Qualification on the AF Form 4418. **(T-2)**

Table 1.1. Crew Position/SMQ Specific Requirements - Written Examinations.

Examination Type	ACD-CC QUAL	ACD-OC QUAL	ACD-O QUAL	*ACD-O/HBS	ACD-O/IRO	*ACD-O/DCC
OPEN BOOK (Note 1)	O	O	O			
CLOSED BOOK (Note 2)	R	R	R			
EPE (Note 3)	R	R	R			
*SMQ CLOSED BOOK (Note 4)				R	R	R

R – required
O – optional

NOTES:
1. Units may administer OPEN BOOK exams at their discretion, however it is not required. If utilized, exams shall consist of 50-100 questions derived from applicable operations manuals and governing directives. OG/OGV will determine the necessary number of questions to be included for each weapon system and crew position. **(T-2)**

2. The CLOSED BOOK exam consists of 25-50 questions derived from applicable operations manuals and governing directives. OG/OGV will determine the necessary number of questions to be included for each weapon system and crew position. **(T-2)**

3. The EPE is required for all INIT QUAL and subsequent periodic QUAL evaluations covering duties in the member's primary crew position. See paragraph 1.5.3 for procedures/requirements for conducting EPEs. **(T-2)**

4. The Special Mission Qualification (SMQ) upgrade CLOSED BOOK exam is a separate closed book exam consisting of 25-50 questions specific to the SMQ derived from applicable operations manuals and governing directives. For initial SMQ evaluations that are not combined with the member's periodic QUAL (for the primary crew position), the SMQ exam is the only required exam. Subsequent (periodic) SMQ evaluations should be combined with the member's periodic QUAL evaluation, therefore, requiring the written requisites to consist of the OPEN BOOK, CLOSED BOOK, and applicable SMQ exam(s). **(T-2)**

1.5.4. QUAL Evaluations. These evaluations measure a crewmember's ability to meet grading areas listed on Table 1.2 at the end of this chapter and defined in Chapter 2 of this instruction. IAW AFI 17-202V2 and weapon system-specific guidance, QUAL evaluations may be combined with MSN evaluations. When practical, QUAL evaluations should be combined with Instructor evaluations, as applicable for the crew position. **(T-2)**

1.5.5. MSN Evaluations. IAW AFI 17-202V2 and lead MAJCOM guidance, the requirement for a separate MSN evaluation may be combined with the QUAL evaluation. The various procedures and techniques used throughout the different weapon system variants are managed through a training program which results in a mission certification or culminates with a SMQ. Mission certifications will be IAW 17-202 Vol 1, AFI 17-2ACD Vol 1, and all applicable supplements and will be documented in the appropriate training folder. MSN and SMQ evaluation grading areas are also listed on Table 1.2 at the end of this chapter and defined in Chapter 2 of this instruction. (T-2)

1.5.5.1. For crew members who maintain multiple mission certifications, recurring evaluations need only evaluate the primary mission events as long as currency is maintained in all other required training events. (T-2)

1.5.6. Instructor Evaluations. Grading areas for these evaluations are listed on Table 1.2 at the end of this chapter. See Chapter 3 of this instruction for amplified information and grading area definitions. (T-2)

1.5.7. SEE Objectivity Evaluations. Grading areas for these evaluations are listed in Table 1.2 at the end of this chapter. See Chapter 4 of this Instruction for amplified information and grading area definitions. (T-2)

1.5.8. No-Notice Evaluations. OG/CC will determine no-notice evaluation procedures/goals. (T-3)

1.6. Grading Instructions. Q, Q- and U ratings are used for specific evaluation areas. Q1, Q2, and Q3 are used for the overall evaluation rating. While the three-level grading system (Q, Q-, U) is used for most areas, a Q- grade will not be used for Critical evaluation areas.

1.6.1. Critical Area/Subarea. Critical areas are events that require adequate accomplishment by the examinee in order to successfully and safely achieve the mission/sortie objectives and complete the evaluation. These events, if not adequately accomplished could result in mission failure, endanger human life, or cause serious injury or death. Additionally, critical areas/subareas apply to time-sensitive tasks or tasks that must be accomplished as expeditiously as possible without any intervening lower priority actions that would, in the normal sequence of events, adversely affect task performance/outcome. If an examinee receives a "U" grade in any critical area, the overall grade for the evaluation will be "Q-3." Critical areas are identified by "(C)" following the applicable area title. (T-2)

1.6.2. Major Area/Subarea. Major areas are events or tasks deemed integral to the performance of other tasks and required to sustain acceptable weapon system operations and mission execution. If an examinee receives a "U" grade in a non-critical area then the overall grade awarded will be no higher than "Q-2." An examinee receiving a "Q-" grade in a non-critical area or areas may still receive a "Q-1" overall grade at evaluator discretion. An overall "Q-3" can be awarded if, in the judgment of the flight examiner, there is justification based on performance in one or several areas/sub areas. Major areas are identified by "(M)" following the applicable area title. (T-2)

1.6.3. Minor Area/Subarea. Minor areas are rudimentary or simple tasks related to weapons system operations that by themselves have little or no impact on mission execution. Minor areas are identified by "(m)" following the applicable area title.

1.6.4. If an examinee receives a "U" grade in a non-critical (major or minor) area then the overall grade awarded will be no higher than "Q-2." An examinee receiving a "Q-" grade in a non-critical area or areas may still receive a "Q-1" overall grade at evaluator discretion. An overall "Q-3" can be awarded if, in the judgment of the SEE, there is justification based on performance in one or several areas/sub areas. **(T-2)**

1.6.5. The SEE must exercise judgment when the wording of areas is subjective and when specific situations are not covered. **(T-2)**

1.6.6. Evaluator judgment will be the final determining factor in deciding the overall qualification level. **(T-2)**

Table 1.2. Crew Position/SMQ Specific Requirements - Performance Phase Evaluations.

AREA/TITLE	Cat	Crew Position						Upgrade	
	C, M, m	ACD-CC	ACD-OC	ACD-O	HBS	IR	DCC	INSTR	SEE
1. Mission Planning	M	R	R	R	R	R	R		
2. Briefing	M	R	R	R	R	R	R		
3. Positional Changeover Brief	M, 1	R	R	R	R	R	R		
4. Safety	C	R	R	R	R	R	R		
5. Emergency Procedures/Equipment	M	R	R	R	R	R	R		
6. Crew Discipline	C	R	R	R	R	R	R		
7. Cyberspace Skills and Knowledge/Situational Awareness	C	R	R	R	R	R	R		
8. Mission Checks/Checklist Procedures	M	R	R	R	R	R	R		
9. Crew Coordination	M	R	R	R	R	R	R		
10. Task Management	M	R	R	R	R	R	R		
11. Systems Knowledge/Operations	M	R	R	R	R	R	R		
12. Communication	M	R	R	R	R	R	R		
13. Reports, Logs, and Forms	M	R	R	R	R	R	R		
14. Post Mission Activity	M	R	R	R	R	R	R		
15. Debrief	M	R	R	R	R	R	R		
16. Mission Management	M	R	R						
17. Composite Force/Mutual Support	M	R	R						
18. Dynamic/Time Sensitive Targeting	M	R	R						
19. Employment Timing	M				R	R	R	R	
20. ACD Collection and Analysis	M			R					
21. HBS Collection and Analysis	M, 2				R				
22. IR Collection and Analysis	M, 2					R			
23. DCC Collection and Analysis	M, 2						R		

24. Cyberspace Interdiction	M, 2					R, 3	R		
25. Cyberspace Strike	M, 2					R, 3	R		
Instructor Upgrade Evaluation Criteria									
26. Instructional Ability	M							R	
27. Instructional Briefings/Critique	M							R	
28. Demonstration and Performance	M							R	
SEE Objectivity Evaluation Criteria									
29. Compliance with Directives	M								R
30. SEE Briefing	M								R
31. Performance Assessment /Grading	M								R
32. Additional Training Assignment	M								R, 4
33. Examinee Debrief	M								R
34. Supervisor Debrief	M								R, 4
35. SEE Performance/Documentation	M								R

C – critical; M – major; m – minor; R – required
NOTES:
1. Applicable for shift/crew changeovers.
2. Grading areas 24 and 25 only apply to those ACD-O crewmembers with the IR SMQ that are selectively designated and qualified to perform additional interdiction and/or strike duties.
3. If required due to examinee's performance.

Chapter 2

CREW POSITION EVALUATIONS AND GRADING CRITERIA

2.1. General. The grading criteria in this chapter apply to evaluations for ACD crew commanders and operations controllers and were established by experience, policies, and procedures set forth in weapon system manuals and other directives. Evaluators must realize that grading criteria contained herein cannot accommodate every situation. Written parameters must be tempered with mission objectives and, more importantly, mission/task accomplishment in the determination of overall crew performance. Requirements for each evaluation are as follows:

2.2. Qualification Evaluations:

2.2.1. Written Examination Requisites: See Table 1.1. **(T-3)**

2.2.2. Emergency Procedures Evaluations: See paragraph 1.5.3. **(T-3)**

2.2.3. Performance Phase: Areas 1 through 19 in Table 1.2 under ACD-CC (Crew Commander qualification) or ACD-OC (Operations Controller qualification) will be evaluated, unless not applicable as noted. **(T-3)**

2.3. Mission Certifications. Mission Certifications ensure that individuals are capable of performing duties essential to the effective employment of the weapon system. Mission Certifications are accomplished IAW local training requirements and/or SQ/CC directions. Mission certification events are normally performed during Qualification evaluations, but may be performed on any mission/sortie with an instructor certified in that mission. **(T-3)**

2.4. General Crew Position Evaluation Criteria. The following general evaluation grading criteria are common to all crew positions, regardless of SMQ and additional certifications, and will be used for all applicable evaluations:

2.4.1. AREA 1, Mission Planning (M)

2.4.1.1. Q. Led or contributed to mission planning efforts IAW procedures prescribed in applicable guidance manuals, instructions, and directives. Planning adequately addressed mission objectives and/or tasking. Plan adequately considered intelligence information, weapon system capability/operating status, and crew composition/ability with minor errors/deviations/omissions that did not impact mission effectiveness. Verified review of all CIF Vol 1, Part B items and complied with Go/No-Go procedures prior to mission start. Was prepared at briefing time. **(T-3)**

2.4.1.2. Q-. Errors/deviations/omissions had minor impact on mission effectiveness or efficiencies, but did not impact mission accomplishment or jeopardize mission success. **(T-3)**

2.4.1.3. U. Failed to adequately lead mission planning effort. Failed to review CIF and/or comply with Go/No-Go procedures. Failures to comply with procedures prescribed in applicable guidance manuals, instructions, and directives contributed to significant deficiencies in mission execution / accomplishment. Failed to lead or participate in all required briefings and/or planning meetings without appropriate approval. **(T-3)**

2.4.2. AREA 2, Briefing (M)

2.4.2.1. Q. Led or contributed to briefing effort as appropriate. Well organized and presented in a logical sequence, appropriate timeframe, and professional manner. Effectively incorporated briefing/training aids and presented all training events and effective techniques required for accomplishing the mission. Briefing encompassed all required topics/areas of discussion IAW prescribed directives. Minor errors/omissions/deviations did not impact mission effectiveness or efficiencies. Crewmembers clearly understood roles, responsibilities, and mission requirements. Briefed CIF Vol 1 Part B and crew Go/No-Go status. **(T-3)**

2.4.2.2. Q-. Led or contributed to briefing effort with minor errors/omissions/deviations. Some events out of sequence with some unnecessary redundancy. Briefing anomalies had minor impact on mission effectiveness but did not jeopardize mission success. **(T-3)**

2.4.2.3. U. Inadequate leadership or participation in briefing development and/or presentation. Disorganized and/or confusing presentation. Ineffective use of briefing/training aids. Failed to brief required topics/discussion areas prescribed in directives. Failed to present major training events. Failed to brief CIF Vol 1 Part B and crew Go/No-Go status. Errors/omissions/deviations impacted crew ability to accomplish the mission. Absent from briefing (whole or in-part) without appropriate supervisor approval. **(T-3)**

2.4.3. AREA 3, Positional Changeover Brief (M)

2.4.3.1. Q. Outgoing crewmember prepared and conducted a comprehensive positional changeover briefing with the oncoming crewmember IAW checklist(s) and applicable directives. Reviewed factors, conditions, and the current operational/tactical situation for all executing packages, sorties, etc. with the oncoming crew member and ensured items necessary for the effective conduct of tasked missions were understood by the oncoming crewmember. Minor errors/omissions/deviations did not impact mission effectiveness. Oncoming crewmember was attentive and asked questions as applicable to ensure mission effectiveness/accomplishment. **(T-3)**

2.4.3.2. Q-. Outgoing crewmember prepared and conducted a positional changeover briefing with minor errors/omissions/deviations using checklist(s) and applicable directives. Changeover briefing anomalies had minor impact on mission effectiveness but did not jeopardize mission success. Oncoming crew member's level of attentiveness during changeover led to minor mission impact but did not jeopardize overall mission success. **(T-3)**

2.4.3.3. U. Outgoing crewmember failed to prepare and conduct an effective positional changeover briefing with the oncoming crewmember and/or failed to use appropriate checklist(s) and applicable directives. Changeover briefing contained errors/omissions/deviations that could have significantly detracted from mission effectiveness and/or jeopardized mission success. Oncoming crew member's lack of attentiveness and/or inadequate requests for clarification could have significantly detracted from mission effectiveness and/or jeopardized mission success. **(T-3)**

2.4.4. AREA 4, Safety (C)

2.4.4.1. Q. Aware of and complied with all factors required for safe operations and mission accomplishment. **(T-3)**

2.4.4.2. U. Was not aware of safety factors or disregarded procedures to safely operate and conduct the mission. Conducted unsafe actions that jeopardized mission accomplishment and/or put crewmembers at risk of injury or death. Operated in a manner that could or did result in damage to the weapon system/equipment. **(T-3)**

2.4.5. AREA 5, Emergency Procedures and Equipment (M)

2.4.5.1. Q. Recognized emergency situations or malfunctions and immediately demonstrated /explained appropriate response actions. Demonstrated/explained thorough knowledge of location and proper use of emergency equipment. Demonstrated/explained effective coordinated emergency actions with other crewmembers without delay or confusion. Followed appropriate checklists as required. [NOTE: Crew Commander is responsible for inspecting/verifying the required contents of the flyaway kit.] Minor errors did not impact efficiencies in addressing the emergency. (This area may be evaluated orally.) **(T-3)**

2.4.5.2. Q-. Recognized emergency situations or malfunctions but slow to demonstrate/explain appropriate response actions. Examinee demonstrated/explained correct procedures with minor errors and/or was slow to locate equipment and/or appropriate checklists. Slow or hesitant to demonstrate/explain coordinated emergency actions with other crewmembers. Minor checklist errors/omissions/deviations caused minor inefficiencies addressing the emergency situation/malfunction but did not exacerbate the situation. **(T-3)**

2.4.5.3. U. Failed to recognize emergency situations or malfunctions. Failed to demonstrate/explain proper response actions. Failed to demonstrate /explain knowledge of location or proper use of emergency equipment or checklists. Failed to demonstrate/explain coordinated emergency actions with other crewmembers. Checklist errors/omissions/deviations contributed to ineffective actions or exacerbating an emergency situation and/or malfunction. **(T-3)**

2.4.6. AREA 6, Crew Discipline (C)

2.4.6.1. Q. Demonstrated strict professional crew discipline throughout all phases of the mission. Planned, briefed, executed, and debriefed mission IAW applicable instructions and directives. **(T-3)**

2.4.6.2. U. Failed to demonstrate strict professional crew discipline throughout all phases of the mission. Violated or failed to comply with applicable instructions and directives which could have jeopardized safety of crewmembers or mission accomplishment. **(T-3)**

2.4.7. AREA 7, Cyberspace Skills and Knowledge/Situational Awareness (C)

2.4.7.1. Q. Conducted the mission with a sense of understanding/comprehension and in a timely, efficient manner. Anticipated situations which would have adversely affected the mission and made appropriate decisions based on available information. Maintained overall good situational awareness. Recognized coordination with intelligence community in order to maintain good situational awareness. Recognized temporary loss of situational awareness in self or others and took appropriate action to regain awareness without detracting from mission accomplishment or jeopardizing safety. **(T-3)**

2.4.7.2. U. Decisions, or lack thereof, resulted in failure to accomplish the assigned mission. Demonstrated poor judgment or lost situational awareness to the extent that safety and/or mission accomplishment could have been compromised. **(T-3)**

2.4.8. AREA 8, Mission Checks/Checklist Procedures (M)

2.4.8.1. Q. Performed all mission/operations checks as required. Efficient location and proficient/timely accomplishment of checklists. Adequately ensured, determined, and/or verified weapon system operational state and crew readiness prior to on-watch period or entering tasked vulnerability period. Ensured crew understanding of most up-to-date tasking(s) prior to on-watch or vulnerability period execution. Deviated from checklists and/or omitted steps only when appropriate and was able to substantiate justification. Minor errors/deviations/omissions did not detract from mission efficiencies nor jeopardize mission success. **(T-3)**

2.4.8.2. Q-. Same as qualified, except minor errors/deviations/omissions detracted from mission efficiencies but did not jeopardize overall mission success. **(T-3)**

2.4.8.3. U. Did not perform mission/operations checks or monitor systems to the degree that an emergency /unsafe condition would have developed or damage to equipment would have occurred if allowed to continue uncorrected. Failed to determine/verify weapon system operational state and crew readiness prior to on-watch period or entering tasked vulnerability period. Unable to locate the appropriate checklist, used incorrect checklist, or consistently omitted checklist items without substantiated justification. Excessive delay in completing required checklist. Errors/deviations/omissions contributed to jeopardizing mission success. **(T-3)**

2.4.9. AREA 9, Crew Coordination (M)

2.4.9.1. Q. Effectively coordinated with other crewmembers during all phases of the mission enabling efficient, well-coordinated actions. Demonstrated basic knowledge of other crewmembers' duties and responsibilities. Proactively provided direction and/or information to the crew; communicated in a clear and effective manner, actively sought other crewmember opinions and/or ideas, and asked for or gave constructive feedback as necessary. **(T-3)**

2.4.9.2. Q-. Some breakdowns in communication but did not detract from overall mission success. Limited in basic knowledge of other crewmembers' duties/responsibilities. Unclear communication at times caused confusion and/or limited crew interaction. Some unnecessary prompting required from other crewmembers. **(T-3)**

2.4.9.3. U. Severe breakdowns in coordination precluded possible mission ineffectiveness/failure or jeopardized safety of crewmembers. Lacked basic knowledge of other crewmember's duties and responsibilities. Unclear/lack of communication or excessive prompting required by crewmembers put mission and/or safety of others at risk. **(T-3)**

2.4.10. AREA 10, Task Management (M)

2.4.10.1. Q. Assured mission success by correctly identifying, prioritizing, and managing tasks based on existing and new information. Used available resources to manage workload and requested assistance when required. Effectively identified contingencies and solutions. Minor errors/omissions but did not result in inefficiencies nor jeopardize mission success. **(T-3)**

2.4.10.2. Q-. Minor omissions and/or errors (which did not affect safety of crewmembers) led to mission inefficiencies but did not jeopardize mission accomplishment. Limited use of available resources to aid decision making, manage workload, and/or slow to request assistance from other crew members when needed. **(T-3)**

2.4.10.3. U. Failed to identify, prioritize, or manage tasks leading to possible unsafe conditions or significant risk to mission accomplishment. Inability to identify contingencies, ineffective decision making, or errors/omissions placed mission accomplishment and/or safety of others at risk. **(T-3)**

2.4.11. AREA 11, Systems Knowledge/Operations (M)

2.4.11.1. Q. Demonstrated thorough knowledge of weapon system components (i.e. equipment, console, applications, tools, and/or software), performance characteristics, employment, and operating procedures. Employed appropriate tactics, techniques, and procedures (TTPs) and made adjustments as necessary throughout all phases of the mission. Correctly identified and applied proper action(s) for system component equipment malfunctions. Followed all applicable system component operating directives, guides, manuals, checklists etc. **(T-3)**

2.4.11.2. Q-. Minor deficiencies or errors resulted in inefficiencies but performance was sufficient to accomplish the mission safely. Did not damage system/components/equipment. **(T-3)**

2.4.11.3. U. Demonstrated severe lack of knowledge of weapon system components/equipment, limitations, performance characteristics, employment or operating procedures. Unable to adequately apply TTPs to accomplish the mission. Failed to identify malfunctions and/or apply corrective actions. Failed to follow system/equipment operating directives, guides, manuals, etc., resulting in unsatisfactory employment. Poor procedures/errors resulted in damage to system components/equipment or jeopardized mission failure. **(T-3)**

2.4.12. AREA 12, Communications (M)

2.4.12.1. Q. Timely and effective communication with external agencies and/or mission partners when required. Concise and accurate information passed using proper medium, terminology, format and/or brevity. Sound understanding and use of voice, email, chat, and collaborative tools to communicate mission essential information. Demonstrated a thorough understanding of Communications Security (COMSEC)/Operations Security (OPSEC) procedures. **(T-3)**

2.4.12.2. Q-. Minor errors/deviations/omissions in communications with external agencies and/or mission partners that did not detract from overall mission accomplishment. Limited understanding and use of voice, email, chat, and collaborative tools. Demonstrated limited understanding of COMSEC/OPSEC procedures with minor errors or deviations that did not jeopardize mission accomplishment. **(T-3)**

2.4.12.3. U. Severe breakdowns in communication with external agencies and/or mission partners created conditions for possible mission ineffectiveness/failure or jeopardized safety of others. Unclear/inaccurate information passed or improper/inadequate use of medium, terminology, format, and/or brevity put mission accomplishment at risk. Significant COMSEC/OPSEC errors or deviations jeopardized mission accomplishment. **(T-3)**

2.4.13. AREA 13, Reports/Logs/Forms (M)

2.4.13.1. Q. Recognized all situations meeting reporting criteria. When required, provided timely, accurate, and correctly formatted reports [e.g. Tactical Reports (TACREPs)/Operational Support Tickets (OSTs), Situation Reports (SITREPs), Mission Reports (MISREPs)] or inputs to mission-related information management portals/collaborative information sharing environments. All required logs [i.e. Master Station Log (MSL)], media and forms were complete, accurate, legible, and accomplished on time and IAW with applicable directives, tasking, and policy. Information was provided in sufficient detail to allow accurate and timely analysis of associated data. Complied with security procedures and directives. **(T-3)**

2.4.13.2. Q-. Minor errors/deviations/omissions/latency on required reports, logs, media, or forms led to minor inefficiencies but did not affect conduct of the mission. Complied with security procedures and directives. **(T-3)**

2.4.13.3. U. Failed to recognize situations meeting reporting criteria and/or failure to report events essential to mission accomplishment. Major errors/deviations/omissions/latency in accomplishing logs, reports/inputs, media, or forms precluded effective mission accomplishment or analysis of mission data. Failed to comply with security procedures and directives. **(T-3)**

2.4.14. AREA 14, Post Mission Activity (M)

2.4.14.1. Q. Accomplished and/or supervised timely post-mission checks, system shutdown procedures, and workstation clean up IAW applicable checklists, guidance, and directives. **(T-3)**

2.4.14.2. Q-. Minor deviations, omissions, or errors but did not adversely impact mission effectiveness, cause damage to systems/equipment, or risk safety of others. **(T-3)**

2.4.14.3. U. Major deviations, omissions, and/or errors were made in performance of post-mission procedures, which could have jeopardized mission effectiveness, caused equipment damage, or endangered others. **(T-3)**

2.4.15. AREA 15, Debrief (M)

2.4.15.1. Q. Thoroughly debriefed the mission and/or contributed to the briefing content to ensure it included all pertinent items. Reconstructed operational events, compared results with initial objectives for the mission, debriefed deviations, and provided individual crew member feedback as appropriate. Organized IAW guidance/directives and professionally presented in a logical sequence using available briefing aids. Summarized lessons learned and ensured they were documented. Provided crew commander/operations controller with applicable input on all required mission/crew/system-related events, including mission log/report/database information for inclusion in the crew debrief. Used applicable checklist(s) as required. Minor errors/omissions/deviations did not impact mission effectiveness or efficiencies. **(T-3)**

2.4.15.2. Q-. Led or contributed to debriefing effort with minor errors/omissions/deviations. Some events out of sequence with some unnecessary redundancy. Briefing or input anomalies had minor impact on mission effectiveness but did not jeopardize mission success. **(T-3)**

2.4.15.3. U. Inadequate leadership or participation in briefing development and/or presentation. Disorganized and/or confusing presentation. Ineffective use of briefing/training aids. Failed to reconstruct operational events, compare results with initial objectives for the mission, debrief deviations, and/or offer corrective guidance as appropriate. Absent from briefing (whole or in-part) without appropriate supervisor approval. Errors, omissions, or deviations jeopardized mission success. **(T-3)**

2.5. Crew Commander (ACD-CC)/Operations Controller (ACD-OC) Specific Evaluation Criteria. The following evaluation grading criteria are common to the Crew Commander and Operations Controller crew positions and will be used for all applicable evaluations. **(T-3)**

2.5.1. AREA 16, Mission Management (M)

2.5.1.1. Q. Assured mission success by accurately identifying, effectively prioritizing, and efficiently managing mission tasks based on planned and updated information. Identified contingencies, gathered data, and formulated decisions. Clearly communicated task priorities and updates to crew members. Used available resources necessary to manage workload, monitor crew activity, and aid in decision making. **(T-3)**

2.5.1.2. Q-. Minor omissions and/or errors which did not affect safety of crewmembers or effective mission accomplishment. Limited use of available resources to aid decision making, manage workload, and/or communicate task priorities/updates to other crew members. **(T-3)**

2.5.1.3. U. Failed to identify, prioritize, or manage mission tasks leading to possible unsafe conditions or significant risk to mission accomplishment. Improperly or unable to identify contingencies, gather data, or communicate decisions putting mission accomplishment and/or safety of others at risk. Failed to communicate task priorities/updates to crew members or adequately monitor crew activity. **(T-3)**

2.5.2. AREA 17, Composite Force/Mutual Support Coordination (M)

2.5.2.1. Q. Effectively planned and integrated with Composite Force (CF) or Mutual Support (MS) agencies to enhance mission effectiveness and achieve objectives. Adhered to all engaged and support contracts and responsibilities. Demonstrated timely coordination with appropriate external agencies. **(T-3)**

2.5.2.2. Q-. Limited planning and/or integration with CF or MS agencies contributed confusion among all or some agencies. Less than optimum mission efficiency however overall mission success was not jeopardized. **(T-3)**

2.5.2.3. U. Inadequate or incorrect planning/integration of CF or MS agencies resulted in mission failure. Demonstrated inadequate knowledge of engaged and support contracts/responsibilities. Late or omitted coordination with appropriate agencies severely degraded or prevented successful mission accomplishment. Did not coordinate or deconflict fire support/weapon system effect delivery with other agencies as required. **(T-3)**

2.5.3. AREA 18, Dynamic/Time Sensitive Targeting (M)

2.5.3.1. Q. Effective coordination with outside agencies and timely contract execution resulted in prompt employment/engagement IAW the Rules of Engagement (ROE), given restrictions or tactical situation. **(T-3)**

2.5.3.2. Q-. Although remaining IAW ROE, minor errors caused delayed contract execution or less than optimal coordination with outside agencies resulted in delayed employment/engagement. **(T-3)**

2.5.3.3. U. Major errors delayed or prevented contract execution and/or resulted in employment/engagement failure. Employment/engagement was outside the ROE, given restrictions, or tactical situation. **(T-3)**

2.6. Employment Timing Specific Evaluation Criteria. The following evaluation grading criteria are common to the ACD-O crew position and crew SMQs for Host Based Security (HBS), Incident Response (IRO), and Defensive Counter Cyberspace (DCC). NOTE: Time will be based on pre-planned Time-on-Target (TOT) for weapon system fire/effect delivery and based on pre-planned vulnerability period for data collection operations. The SEE may widen TOT, vulnerability period, and/or push times grading criteria if the examinee was forced to delay due to factors beyond the examinee's control such as weapon system maintenance/malfunctions, adversary activity, outside agency errors or non-availability, re-tasking, employment contingencies, etc. Evaluate all briefed mission timings (fence/pre-on watch checks, ingress/egress times, vulnerability period, time on target, etc.). **(T-3)**

2.6.1. AREA 19, Employment Timing (M)

2.6.1.1. Q. Effectively met mission timings and accomplished 80% or greater of all tasking within assigned TOT/Vulnerability Period/Push Time window. **(T-3)**

2.6.1.2. Q-. Minor errors but effectively met most mission timings; accomplished at least 60% to 80% of tasking within assigned TOT/Vulnerability Period/Push Time. **(T-3)**

2.6.1.3. U. Unable to meet critical mission timing requirements resulting in severe degradation or failure of the mission. Failed to meet Q- requirements for meeting TOT/Vulnerability Period/Push Time and tasking accomplishment threshold. **(T-3)**

2.7. ACD-Operator (ACD-O) Specific Evaluation Criteria. The following evaluation grading criteria is for the ACD-O crew position and will be used for all applicable evaluations:

2.7.1. AREA 20, ACD Collection and Analysis (M)

2.7.1.1. Q. Properly planned and executed collection, correlation, categorization and storage of network security events IAW tasking, directives, and applicable checklists. Demonstrated thorough knowledge in procedures and techniques for monitoring/reviewing alerts and analyzing data to identify potential malicious traffic. Correctly recognized, identified, and categorized suspicious activities/events requiring further analysis and investigation. **(T-3)**

2.7.1.2. Q-. Minor errors, omissions, or delays detracted from mission efficiency but did not jeopardize overall mission accomplishment. **(T-3)**

2.7.1.3. U. Errors, omissions, or delays jeopardized overall mission accomplishment. **(T-3)**

2.8. Host Based Security (HBS) SMQ Specific Evaluation Criteria. The following evaluation grading criteria is for the HBS special mission qualification and will be used for all applicable evaluations:

2.8.1. AREA 21, HBS Collection and Analysis (M)

2.8.1.1. Q. Properly planned and executed optimized queries to collect, correlate, categorize and store network security events IAW tasking, directives, and applicable checklists. Demonstrated thorough knowledge in procedures and techniques for reviewing query results and analyzing data. Correctly recognized, identified, and categorized suspicious or malicious activities/events requiring further analysis and investigation. **(T-3)**

2.8.1.2. Q-. Minor errors, omissions, or delays detracted from mission efficiency but did not jeopardize overall mission accomplishment. **(T-3)**

2.8.1.3. U. Errors, omissions, or delays jeopardized overall mission accomplishment. **(T-3)**

2.9. Incident Response (IRO) SMQ Specific Evaluation Criteria. The following evaluation grading criteria is for the IR special mission qualification and will be used for all applicable evaluations:

2.9.1. AREA 22, IR Collection and Analysis (M)

2.9.1.1. Q. Properly planned and executed remote scan/access of identified and/or prioritized enterprise hosts IAW tasking, directives, procedures, and applicable checklists. Demonstrated thorough knowledge of procedures and techniques for analyzing specified system hard drives, operating systems, registries, connected peripherals, and memory for abnormal artifacts or potentially malicious activity. Able to differentiate between events and incidents. Demonstrated thorough knowledge in procedures and techniques for analyzing end-user provided Windows OS/*NIX systems and forensic tool output data. **(T-3)**

2.9.1.2. Q-. Minor errors, omissions, or delays detracted from mission efficiency but did not jeopardize overall mission accomplishment. **(T-3)**

2.9.1.3. U. Errors, omissions, or delays jeopardized overall mission accomplishment. **(T-3)**

2.10. Defensive Counter Cyberspace (DCC) SMQ Specific Evaluation Criteria. The following evaluation grading criteria is for the DCC special mission qualification and will be used for all applicable evaluations:

2.10.1. AREA 23, DCC Collection and Analysis (M)

2.10.1.1. Q. Properly planned and executed remote scan/access of identified and/or prioritized enterprise hosts IAW tasking, directives, procedures, and applicable checklists. Demonstrated thorough knowledge of procedures and techniques for analyzing specified system hard drives, operating systems, registries, connected peripherals, and memory for abnormal artifacts or potentially malicious activity. Demonstrated thorough knowledge in procedures and techniques for accessing and analyzing Windows OS/UNIX systems and forensic tool output data. **(T-3)**

2.10.1.2. Q-. Minor errors, omissions, or delays detracted from mission efficiency but did not jeopardize overall mission accomplishment. **(T-3)**

2.10.1.3. U. Errors, omissions, or delays jeopardized overall mission accomplishment. **(T-3)**

2.11. Interdiction/Strike Evaluation Criteria. The following evaluation grading criteria apply to all DCC special mission qualified crewmembers and select/designated IR special mission qualified crewmembers:

2.11.1. AREA 24, Cyberspace Interdiction (M)

2.11.1.1. Q. Properly planned and executed interdiction of validated targets IAW tasking, directives, and applicable checklists. Demonstrated thorough knowledge of tactics, techniques, and procedures for denying, degrading, or disrupting adversary process, code, command and control, communication, sensing, storage and access capabilities. Actions were appropriate to affect the terrain based on the validated target's characteristics and IAW the Standing ROE (SROE), Pre-Approved Actions (PAAs), mission tasking, and intended effect. **(T-3)**

2.11.1.2. Q-. Minor errors, omissions, or delays detracted from mission efficiency but did not jeopardize overall mission accomplishment. **(T-3)**

2.11.1.3. U. Errors, omissions, or delays jeopardized overall mission accomplishment. **(T-3)**

2.11.2. AREA 25, Cyberspace Strike (M)

2.11.2.1. Q. Properly planned and executed strike(s) on validated targets IAW tasking, directives, and applicable checklists. Demonstrated thorough knowledge of tactics, techniques, and procedures for destroying specified targets, to include direct action on malicious process, code, logs, and remnants. Actions were appropriate for the target (while preserving the terrain) based on the validated target's characteristics and IAW the SROE, PAAs, mission tasking, and/or intended effect. **(T-3)**

2.11.2.2. Q-. Minor errors, omissions, or delays detracted from mission efficiency but did not jeopardize overall mission accomplishment. **(T-3)**

2.11.2.3. U. Errors, omissions, or delays jeopardized overall mission accomplishment. **(T-3)**

Chapter 3

INSTRUCTOR EVALUATIONS AND GRADING CRITERIA

3.1. General. Grading criteria contained herein cannot accommodate every situation. Written parameters must be tempered with sortie objectives, evaluator judgment, and task accomplishment in the determination of overall crew performance. **(T-2)**

3.2. Instructor Upgrade and Qualification Requisites. Prior to an initial Instructor Evaluation, Instructor examinees must complete all requisites for Instructor upgrade consideration, nomination and training IAW AFI 17-202, Vol 1, AFI 17-2ACD, Vol 1, and all applicable supplemental guidance. **(T-2)**

3.3. Instructor Qualification Evaluations: When possible, units should strive to combine instructor evaluations (initial and recurring/periodic) with periodic QUAL evaluations. Instructor evaluations can only be combined with QUAL evaluations when the examinee is in their periodic QUAL eligibility period. There is no eligibility period associated with an Instructor Qualification, however, Instructor qualifications will expire after the 17th month from the previous Instructor Qualification Evaluation. See paragraph 3.5 for documentation guidance. **(T-2)**

3.3.1. Initial Instructor evaluations should be conducted with a student occupying the applicable crew position whenever possible. Recurring or periodic Instructor Evaluations may be conducted with the SEE role playing as the student. **(T-2)**

3.3.2. The instructor examinee will monitor all phases of the mission from an advantageous position and be prepared to demonstrate or explain any area or procedure. The SEE will particularly note the instructor's ability to recognize student difficulties and provide effective, timely instruction and/or corrective action. The SEE should also evaluate the grade assigned and the completed grade sheet or event training form for the student on all initial instructor checks. **(T-2)**

3.3.3. The student will perform those duties prescribed by the instructor for the mission/sortie being accomplished. If an actual student is not available, the SEE will identify to the examinee (prior to the mission) the level of performance expected from the SEE acting as the student. If this option is utilized, at least one event or briefing must be instructed. **(T-2)**

3.3.4. Periodic instructor evaluations will be administered in conjunction with required periodic qualification evaluations. The examinee must occupy the primary duty position for an adequate period of time to demonstrate proficiency in the crew position with required qualification evaluations. All instructor evaluations will include a pre-mission and post-mission briefing. **(T-2)**

3.3.5. Awarding a "U" in any of the Instructor Grading Criteria areas will result in a Q-3 for the overall instructor grade. The overall grade for the instructor portion of the evaluation will be no higher than the lowest overall grade awarded under QUAL. **(T-2)**

3.4. Instructor Evaluation Grading Criteria. All Instructor Evaluation Criteria must be observed and graded to ensure a complete evaluation. Specific requirements for each evaluation are as follows:

3.4.1. AREA 26, Instructional Ability (M)

3.4.1.1. Q. Demonstrated ability to communicate effectively. Provided appropriate corrective guidance when necessary. Planned ahead and made timely decisions. Correctly analyzed student errors. **(T-2)**

3.4.1.2. Q-. Minor discrepancies in the above criteria that did not adversely impact student progress. **(T-2)**

3.4.1.3. U. Unable to effectively communicate with the student. Did not provide corrective action where necessary. Did not plan ahead or anticipate student problems. Incorrectly analyzed student errors. Adversely impacted student progress. **(T-2)**

3.4.2. AREA 27, Instructional Briefings/Critique (M)

3.4.2.1. Q. Briefings were well organized, accurate, and thorough. Reviewed student's present level of training and defined mission events to be performed. Demonstrated ability during critique to reconstruct the mission/sortie, offer mission analysis, and provide corrective guidance where appropriate. Completed all training documents according to prescribed directives. Appropriate grades awarded. **(T-2)**

3.4.2.2. Q-. As above but with minor errors or omissions in briefings, critique, or training documents that did not adversely impact student progress. **(T-2)**

3.4.2.3. U. Pre-mission or post-mission briefings were marginal or nonexistent. Did not review student's training folder or past performance. Failed to adequately critique student or conducted an incomplete mission analysis which compromised learning. Student strengths or weaknesses were not identified. Adversely impacted student progress. Inappropriate grades awarded. Overlooked or omitted major discrepancies. **(T-2)**

3.4.3. AREA 28, Demonstration and Performance (M)

3.4.3.1. Q. Effectively demonstrated procedures and techniques. Demonstrated thorough knowledge of weapon system/components, procedures, and all applicable publications and regulations. **(T-2)**

3.4.3.2. Q-. Minor discrepancies in the above criteria that did not adversely impact student progress. **(T-2)**

3.4.3.3. U. Did not demonstrate correct procedure or technique. Insufficient depth of knowledge about weapon system/components, procedures, or proper source material. Adversely impacted student progress. **(T-2)**

3.5. Instructor Evaluation Documentation.

3.5.1. Instructor Qualification Evaluations will be documented as a SPOT evaluation on the AF Form 4418 and AF Form 4420, *Individual's Record of Duties and Qualifications*, and maintained in the member's crew qualification folder IAW AFI 17-202, Vol 2, applicable higher headquarters supplements, and local supplemental guidance. **(T-2)** Additional Instructor Evaluation documentation is as follows:

3.5.2. Initial Instructor Qualification Evaluation.

3.5.2.1. If conducted in conjunction with the Instructor Examinee's periodic QUAL evaluation, the Instructor Qualification Evaluation will be documented on the same AF Form 4418, placing SPOT in the second "Evaluation Type" block of Section II Qualification below annotating QUAL. Place a statement in Section V Comments that the QUAL evaluation was in conjunction with an Initial Instructor Qualification Evaluation. Place any comments specific to the Instructor portion of the evaluation separately from the QUAL portion of the evaluation. **(T-2)**

3.5.2.2. If the Instructor Qualification Evaluation is not in conjunction with a periodic QUAL evaluation, document the evaluation as a SPOT in the first "Evaluation Type" block of Section II Qualification and place a statement in Section V Comments that the evaluation was an Initial Instructor Qualification Evaluation. Place any comments regarding commendable performance and/or discrepancies for the instructor evaluation in Section V Comments. **(T-2)**

3.5.2.3. Upon completion of the AF Form 4418, place the appropriate corresponding entry onto the AF Form 4420.

3.5.3. Recurring/Periodic Instructor Qualification Evaluation.

3.5.3.1. If conducted in conjunction with the Instructor Examinee's periodic QUAL evaluation, the Instructor Qualification Evaluation will be documented on the same AF Form 4418, placing SPOT in the second "Evaluation Type" block of Section II Qualification below annotating QUAL. Place a statement in Section V Comments that the evaluation was a periodic QUAL evaluation in conjunction with periodic or recurring Instructor Qualification Evaluation. Place any comments specific to the Instructor portion of the evaluation separately from the QUAL portion of the evaluation. **(T-2)**

3.5.3.2. If the Instructor Qualification Evaluation is not in conjunction with a periodic QUAL evaluation, document the evaluation as a SPOT in the first "Evaluation Type" block of Section II Qualification and place a statement in Section V Comments that the evaluation was recurring or periodic Instructor Qualification Evaluation. Place any comments regarding commendable performance and/or discrepancies for the instructor evaluation in Section V Comments. **(T-2)**

3.5.3.3. Upon completion of the AF Form 4418, place the appropriate corresponding entry onto the AF Form 4420. **(T-2)**

3.5.4. Letter of Certification.

3.5.4.1. The Letter of Certification is the list of all the certifications and qualifications for MR and BMC personnel within the unit. The Letter of Certification is maintained by the unit and is signed by the unit commander. **(T-2)**

3.5.4.2. Upon the successful completion of an Instructor Qualification Evaluation, units will ensure the crewmembers instructor status is reflected on the Letter of Certification. **(T-2)**

3.5.4.3. Upon the expiration of a qualification or failure of an Instructor Qualification Evaluation, units will ensure the crewmembers instructor status is reflected on the Letter of Certification. **(T-2)**

Chapter 4

SEE OBJECTIVITY EVALUATIONS AND GRADING CRITERIA

4.1. General. SEE Objectivity Evaluations are a vehicle for commanders to upgrade crewmembers for SEE qualification and a tool to monitor the evaluator crew force's adherence to Stan/Eval directives. Grading criteria contained herein cannot accommodate every situation. Written parameters must be tempered with sortie objectives, evaluator judgment, and task accomplishment in the determination of overall examinee performance. The criteria contained in this chapter are established by experience, policies, and procedures set forth in weapon system manuals and other directives. The criteria contained in this chapter are applicable to all SEE Objectivity Evaluations for ACD crewmembers. **(T-2)**

4.2. Evaluator Upgrade and Qualification Requisites. Evaluator upgrade candidates will be selected from the most qualified and competent instructors. **(T-2)**

4.2.1. Wing/Group/Squadron. SEE Upgrade candidate nominations will be approved by the OG/CC in writing. Once approved, candidates must complete all SEE training IAW AFI 17-202, Vol 2, this instruction, and all applicable supplemental guidance. **(T-2)** As a minimum, SEE training will consist of:

4.2.1.1. Local SEE academics/instruction covering all Stan/Eval programs and procedures. Training completion should be documented on a locally developed OG/CC checklist along with a signed certificate from the OG/CC or OG/CD. Both checklist and certificate will be maintained in the unit Stan/Eval office. **(T-2)**

4.2.1.2. The candidate observing one entire evaluation performed by a qualified SEE. NOTE: To the maximum extent possible, SEE Upgrade candidates should observe evaluations conducted within the weapon system for which they are qualified, however when not practical, the observed evaluation may be conducted with a qualified SEE within in the same Group regardless of weapon system or crew position. Training completion should be documented on a locally developed OG/CC checklist and maintained in the unit Stan/Eval office. **(T-2)**

4.2.1.3. Completion of a SEE Objectivity Evaluation under the supervision of a qualified SEE. NOTE: The SEE Objectivity Evaluation will be conducted within the weapon system and crew position for which the SEE Upgrade candidate (SEE Examinee) maintains qualification. See paragraph 4.5 for SEE Objectivity Evaluation (AF Form 4418) documentation guidance. **(T-2)**

4.3. SEE Objectivity Evaluations. There is no eligibility period or expiration date associated with a SEE Objectivity Evaluation. Once obtained, crewmembers maintain SEE qualification unless they fail a QUAL evaluation, fail an Instructor evaluation, fail a SEE Objectivity Evaluation, their weapon system QUAL expires, or upon their SEE appointment being revoked/rescinded by the appointing official. See paragraph 4.5 for SEE Objectivity Evaluation documentation guidance. **(T-2)**

4.3.1. Only a qualified cyberspace weapon system SEE may administer a SEE Objectivity Evaluation to a cyberspace SEE examinee. SEE Objectivity Evaluations may be administered by SEE Examiners qualified in a different cyberspace weapon system type or crew position from the SEE examinee. NOTE: This is common when the SEE Objectivity Evaluation is in conjunction with a higher headquarters inspection. **(T-2)**

4.3.2. SEE Objectivity Evaluations will not be combined with any other type evaluation. **(T-2)**

4.3.3. SEE Objectivity Evaluations will ensure the SEE examinee (for example in the case of a SEE Objectivity conducted as part of a higher headquarters inspection) observes and grades the entire mission activity of the QUAL examinee. Mission activity is defined as all mission planning, briefing, execution, and debrief activities for the mission/sortie. **(T-2)**

4.3.4. The SEE Upgrade candidate or SEE Examinee will brief the qualified SEE Examiner on all observations, grades, commendable/discrepancies (if any), recommended additional training, and other mission related debrief topics prior to debriefing the QUAL examinee and/or examinee's supervisor. **(T-2)**

4.3.5. The SEE Upgrade candidate or SEE Examinee will complete the AF Form 4418 and have the SEE Examiner review it for completeness and accuracy. The SEE Examiner's signature block and signature (not signature/block of the SEE Upgrade candidate or SEE Examinee) will be entered on the AF Form 4418. **(T-2)**

4.3.6. The SEE Examiner will administer a pre-brief and debrief to the SEE Examinee. **(T-2)**

4.3.7. For SEE Upgrade candidates, SEE Objectivity evaluations will only be administered for observed INIT QUAL or periodic QUAL evaluations. Additionally, the QUAL evaluation may not be combined with an Instructor Evaluation. **(T-2)**

4.4. SEE Objectivity Evaluation Grading Criteria. All SEE Objectivity Evaluation Criteria must be observed and graded to ensure a complete evaluation. The following grading criteria will be used by SEE's when conducting SEE Objectivity Evaluations. A grade of Q- requiring additional training or a grade of U in any area for the SEE Objectivity Examinee will require an overall rating of "3". Cumulative deviations will be considered when determining the overall rating of either "1" or "3". **(T-2)**Specific requirements for each evaluation are as follows:

4.4.1. AREA 29, Compliance with Directives (M)

4.4.1.1. Q. Complied with all operational directives and guidance. Complied with all directives pertaining to the administration of a positional and/or instructor evaluation. **(T-2)**

4.4.1.2. Q-. Complied with most directives. Deviations did not jeopardize the mission, the effectiveness of the evaluation, or crew safety. **(T-2)**

4.4.1.3. U. Failure to comply with directives jeopardized mission effectiveness, effectiveness of the evaluation, and/or crew safety. **(T-2)**

4.4.2. AREA 30, Stan/Eval Examiner (SEE) Briefing (M)

4.4.2.1. Q. Thoroughly briefed the examinee on the conduct of the evaluation, mission requirements, responsibilities, grading criteria, and examiner actions/position during the evaluation. **(T-2)**

4.4.2.2. Q-. Items were omitted during the briefing causing minor confusion. Did not fully brief the examinee as to the conduct and purpose of the evaluation. **(T-2)**

4.4.2.3. U. Examiner failed to adequately brief the examinee. **(T-2)**

4.4.3. AREA 31, Performance Assessment and Grading (M)

4.4.3.1. Q. Identified all discrepancies and assigned proper area grade. Awarded the appropriate overall grade based on the examinee's performance. **(T-2)**

4.4.3.2. Q-. Most discrepancies were identified. Failed to assign Q- grade when appropriate. Assigned discrepancies for performance which was within standards. Awarded an overall grade without consideration of cumulative deviations in the examinee's performance. **(T-2)**

4.4.3.3. U. Failed to identify most discrepancies. Did not award a grade commensurate with overall performance. Failed to assign additional training when warranted. **(T-2)**

4.4.4. AREA 32, Additional Training Assignment (M)

4.4.4.1. Q. Assigned proper additional training when warranted. NOTE: If the QUAL Examinee's performance (i.e. Q1) does not warrant the assignment of additional training, the SEE Examinee will verbally explain to the SEE Examiner the proper procedures for assigning additional training. This may be accomplished as part of the SEE Objectivity pre-brief or debrief. **(T-2)**

4.4.4.2. Q-. Additional training assigned was insufficient to ensure the examinee would achieve proper level of qualification. SEE Examinee's discrepancy or omission was correctable prior to QUAL Examinee debrief and in the SEE Objectivity debrief. **(T-2)**

4.4.4.3. U. Failed to assign additional training when warranted. **(T-2)**

4.4.5. AREA 33, Examinee Critique / Debrief (M)

4.4.5.1. Q. Thoroughly debriefed the examinee on all aspects of the evaluation. Reconstructed and debriefed all key mission events, providing instruction and references to directives and guidance when applicable. **(T-2)**

4.4.5.2. Q-. Some errors/omissions in reconstructing key mission events, in discussing deviations/discrepancies, referencing directives/guidance and debriefing of assigned grades. Did not advise the examinee of all additional training when warranted. Errors/omissions did not adversely affect overall evaluation effectiveness. **(T-2)**

4.4.5.3. U. Failed to discuss any assigned area grades or the overall rating. Changed grades without briefing the examinee and/or supervisor. Did not debrief key mission events and/or provide appropriate instruction during critique. **(T-2)**

4.4.6. AREA 34, Supervisor Debrief (M)

4.4.6.1. Q. Thoroughly debriefed the QUAL Examinee. Reconstructed and debriefed all key mission events pertinent to the QUAL Examinee's performance, citing references to directives and guidance when applicable. Briefed the supervisor on all discrepancies requiring additional training, downgraded areas, and the overall qualification rating assigned to the QUAL Examinee. NOTE: If the QUAL Examinee's performance (i.e. Q1) does not warrant a supervisor debrief, the SEE Examinee will verbally explain to the SEE

Examiner the proper procedures for conducting a supervisor debriefing. This may be accomplished as part of the SEE Objectivity pre-brief or debrief. **(T-2)**

4.4.6.2. Q-. Some errors/omissions in reconstructing key mission events, discussing deviations/discrepancies, referencing directives/guidance, debriefing of assigned additional training, and assigning of QUAL Examinee grades/ratings with the supervisor. Errors/omissions did not adversely affect overall evaluation effectiveness. **(T-2)**

4.4.6.3. U. Failed to discuss any observed discrepancies, assigned area downgrades or the overall rating with the supervisor. Changed grades without briefing the examinee and/or supervisor. Did not debrief key mission events contributing to the QUAL examinees overall performance and assigned qualification rating. **(T-2)**

4.4.7. AREA 35, SEE Performance and Evaluation Documentation (M)

4.4.7.1. Q. SEE Examinee performed as briefed and ensured a thorough evaluation of the QUAL and/or Instructor (INSTR) evaluation examinee. SEE Examinee correctly documented the QUAL or INSTR Examinee's performance on the AF Form 4418. **(T-2)**

4.4.7.2. Q-. Minor errors or discrepancies during the mission did not impact or detract from the QUAL or INSTR Examinees' performance. Minor errors/discrepancies in accomplishing documentation. **(T-2)**

4.4.7.3. U. Major errors/disruptions impacted or detracted from the QUAL or INSTR Examinee's performance and/or prevented a thorough evaluation. Failure or major errors/discrepancies in accomplishing documentation. **(T-2)**

4.5. SEE Objectivity Evaluation Documentation. SEE Objectivity Evaluations will be documented as a SPOT evaluation on the AF Form 4418 and AF Form 4420 and maintained in the member's crew qualification folder IAW AFI 17-202 Vol 2 and applicable higher headquarters/local supplemental guidance. **(T-2)**

4.5.1. Letter of Certification.

4.5.1.1. Upon the successful completion of a SEE Objectivity Evaluation, units will ensure the crewmembers SEE status is reflected on the Letter of Certification. **(T-2)**

4.5.1.2. Upon the decertification or loss of SEE qualification, units will ensure the Letter of Certification appropriately reflects the crewmember's status. **(T-2)**

WILLIAM J. BENDER, Lt Gen, USAF
Chief of Information Dominance and Chief
Information Officer

Attachment 1

GLOSSARY OF REFERENCES AND SUPPORTING INFORMATION

References

AFPD 17-2, *Cyberspace Operations*, 12 April 2016

AFI 17-202 V1, *Cybercrew Training*, 2 April 2014

AFI 17-202 V2, *Cybercrew Standardization and Evaluation Program*, 15 October 2014

AFI 17-202 V3, *Cyberspace Operations and Procedures*, 15 February 2014

AFI 17-2ACD Volume 1, *Air Force Cyberspace Defense (ACD) Training*

AFI 33-360, *Publications and Forms Management*, 1 December 2015

AFMAN 33-363, *Management of Records*, 1 March 2008

Prescribed Forms

None

Adopted Forms

AF Form 847, *Recommendation for Change of Publication*

AF Form 4418, *Certificate of Cybercrew Qualification*

AF Form 4420, *Individual's Record of Duties and Qualifications*

Abbreviations and Acronyms

AF—Air Force

AFI—Air Force Instruction

ACD—Air Force Cyberspace Defense

ACD-CC – Air Force Cyberspace Defense Crew Commander

ACD-OC – Air Force Cyberspace Defense Operations Controller

ACD-O – Air Force Cyberspace Defense Operator

AFMAN—Air Force Manual

AFPD—Air Force Policy Directive

AFRC—Air Force Reserve Command

AFRIMS—Air Force Records Management Information System

AFSPC—Air Force Space Command

ANG—Air National Guard

CCC—Crew Commander

CF—Composite Force

CIF—Crew Information Folder

CTD—Crew Training Device

DCC—Defensive Counter Cyberspace

EPE—Emergency Procedure Evaluation

HBS—Host Based Security

HQ—Headquarters

IAW—In Accordance With

INSTR—Instructor

IRO—Incident Response

LEP—List of Effective Pages

MAJCOM—Major Command

MISREP—Mission Report

MS—Mutual Support

MSL—Master Station Log

MSN—Mission Qualification

MTTL—Master Training Task List

NAF—Numbered Air Force

N/N—No-notice

OC—Operations Controller

OG—Operations Group

OG/CC—Operations Group Commander

OGV—Operations Group Standardization/Evaluation

OPR—Office of Primary Responsibility

OST—Operational Support Ticket

PAA – Pre-Approved Action

QUAL—Qualification

RDS—Records Disposition Schedule

ROE—Rules of Engagement

SEE—Stan/Eval Examiner

SITREP—Situation Report

SPOT—Spot Evaluation

SQ—Squadron

SROE—Standing Rules of Engagement

STAN/EVAL—Standardization and Evaluation

TACREP—Tactical Report

TDY—Temporary Duty

TOT—Time on Target

Terms

Airmanship—A crew member's continuous perception of self and weapon system/mission equipment in relation to the dynamic environment of operations, threats, and tasking, and the ability to forecast and execute tasks based on that perception.

Commendable—An observed exemplary demonstration of knowledge and/or or noteworthy ability to perform by the examinee in a particular graded area/subarea, tactic, technique, procedure, and/or task.

Crew Commander (CCC)—Cyberspace operator qualified to perform crew commander duties.

Crew Training Devices—All trainers, computer assisted instruction, sound-on-slide programs, videos, and mockups designed to prepare students for operations training or augment prescribed continuation training.

Deficiency—Demonstrated level of knowledge or ability to perform is inadequate, insufficient, or short of meeting required or expected proficiency.

Deviation—Performing an action not in sequence with current procedures, directives, or regulations. Performing action(s) out of sequence due to unusual or extenuating circumstances is not considered a deviation. In some cases, momentary deviations may be acceptable; however, cumulative deviations will be considered in determining the overall qualification level.

Discrepancy—Any observed deviations/errors/omissions, individually or cumulative, that detracts from the examinee's performance in obtaining a Q for a particular grading area/subarea.

Error—Departure from standard procedure. Performing incorrect actions or recording inaccurate information.

Stan/Eval Examiner (SEE)—A crew member designated to administer evaluations.

Inadequate—Lack or underutilization of available crew aids or resources to effectively/efficiently make operational and tactical decisions, gain/maintain situational awareness, or accomplish a task.

Inappropriate—Excessive reliance on crew aids/other resources or utilizing a crew aid/ resource outside its intended use.

Instructor—Crew member trained, qualified, and certified by the squadron commander as an instructor to perform both ground and in-flight training.

Instructor Supervision—When a current instructor, who is qualified in the same crew position, supervises a maneuver or training event.

Major (deviation/error/omission)—Detracted from task accomplishment, adversely affected use of equipment, or violated safety.

Minor (deviation/error/omission)—Did not detract from task accomplishment, adversely affect use of equipment, or violate safety.

Omission—To leave out a required action or annotation.

Operations Controller (OC)—Cyberspace operator qualified to perform operations controller duties.

Supervised Training Status—Crew member will perform weapon system duties under instructor supervision as designated by the squadron commander or evaluator.

BY ORDER OF THE SECRETARY
OF THE AIR FORCE

AIR FORCE INSTRUCTION 17-2ACD
VOLUME 3

27 APRIL 2017

Cyberspace

AIR FORCE CYBERSPACE
DEFENSE (ACD)
OPERATIONS AND PROCEDURES

COMPLIANCE WITH THIS PUBLICATION IS MANDATORY

ACCESSIBILITY: Publications and forms are available on the Publishing website at www.e-Publishing.af.mil for downloading or ordering

RELEASABILITY: There are no releasability restrictions on this publication

OPR: HQ USAF/A3CX/A6CX

Certified by: HQ USAF/A3C/A6C
(Brig Gen Kevin B. Kennedy)
Pages: 24

This volume implements Air Force (AF) Policy Directive (AFPD) 17-2, *Cyberspace Operations* and references AFI 17-202V3, *Cyberspace Operations and Procedures.* It applies to all AF Cyberspace Defense (ACD) units. This publication applies to all military and civilian AF personnel, members of the AF Reserve Command (AFRC), Air National Guard (ANG), and contractor support personnel in accordance with appropriate provisions contained in memoranda support agreements and AF contracts. This publication requires the collection and or maintenance of information protected by the Privacy Act (PA) of 1947. The authorities to collect and maintain the records prescribed in this publication are Title 10 United States Code, **Chapter 857** and Executive Order 9397, Numbering System for Federal Accounts Relating to Individual Persons, 30 November 1943, as amended by Executive Order 13478, Amendments to Executive Order 9397 Relating to Federal Agency Use of Social Security Numbers, November 18, 2008.

The authorities to waive wing/unit level requirements in this publication are identified with a Tier ("T-0, T-1, T-2, T-3") number following the compliance statement. See AFI 33-360, *Publications and Forms Management*, Table 1.1 for a description of the authorities associated with the Tier numbers. Submit requests for waivers through the chain of command to the appropriate Tier waiver approval authority, or alternately, to the publication OPR for non-tiered compliance items. Refer recommended changes and questions about this publication to the Office of Primary Responsibility (OPR) using AF Form 847, *Recommendation for Change of Publication*; route AF Forms 847 from the field through Major Command (MAJCOM) publications/forms managers to AF/A3C/A6C. Ensure all records created as a result of processes prescribed in this publication are maintained in accordance with AF Manual (AFMAN) 33-363, *Management of Records* and disposed of in accordance with (IAW) the AF Records Disposition Schedule (RDS) located in the AF Records Management Information System (AFRIMS).

Chapter 1

GENERAL GUIDANCE

1.1. References, Abbreviations, Acronyms, and Terms. See Attachment 1

1.2. General. This volume, in conjunction with other governing directives, prescribes procedures for operating the ACD weapon system under most circumstances. It is not a substitute for sound judgment or common sense. Procedures not specifically addressed may be accomplished if they enhance safe and effective mission accomplishment.

1.3. Waivers. Unless another approval authority is cited ("T-0, T-1, T-2, T-3"), waiver authority for this volume is the MAJCOM/A3 (or equivalent). Submit requests for waivers using AF Form 679 through the chain of command to the appropriate Tier waiver approval authority. If approved, waivers remain in effect for the life of the published guidance, unless the waiver authority specifies a shorter period of time, cancels in writing, or issues a change that alters the basis for the waiver.

1.4. Deviations. In the case of an urgent requirement or emergency the Crew Commander (ACD-CC) will take appropriate action(s) to ensure safe operations. **(T-3)**

1.5. Processing Changes

1.5.1. Submit recommended changes and questions about this publication through MAJCOM channels to the OPR using AF Form 847. **(T-2)**

1.5.2. The submitting MAJCOM will forward information copies of AF Forms 847 to all other MAJCOMS that use this publication. Using MAJCOMs will forward comments on AF Form 847 to the OPR. **(T-2)**

1.5.3. OPR will:

1.5.3.1. Coordinate all changes to the basic instruction with HQ AFSPC/A2/3/6. **(T-2)**

1.5.3.2. Forward change recommendations to HQ AFSPC/A2/3/6 for staffing and forwarding to AF/A3 for approval. **(T-2)**

1.6. Supplements. Guidance for supplementing this publication is contained in AFI 33-360. Supplements will not duplicate, alter, amend or be less restrictive than the provisions of this Instruction. **(T-2)**

Chapter 2

MISSION PLANNING

2.1. Responsibilities. Individual crews, unit operations, and intelligence functions share responsibility for mission planning. The ACD-CC is ultimately responsible for all tactical aspects of mission planning to include complying with command guidance. Unit commanders may supplement mission planning requirements but will ensure an appropriate level of mission planning is conducted prior to each mission. **(T-3)**

2.2. Mission Planning Guidelines.

2.2.1. Effective mission accomplishment requires thorough mission planning and preparation. Specific mission planning elements are addressed in Air Force Tactics, Techniques, and Procedures (AFTTP) 3-1.General Planning, AFTTP 3-1.ACD, Air Forces Cyber (AFCYBER) & Joint Forces Headquarters-Cyber (JFHQ-C) AFCYBER Tactical Mission Planning, Briefing and Debriefing Guide, and any local crew aids. While not directive, these manuals are authoritative and useful in ensuring adequate mission planning and employment. **(T-3)**

2.2.2. Standard Operating Procedures (SOP). The squadron (SQ) commander (SQ/CC) is the approval authority for squadron standards. The operations group (OG) commander (OG/CC) may publish and approve group standards. The OG Standardization and Evaluation office (OGV) will review all standards for compliance with AFI 17-series guidance. **(T-3)**

2.2.3. Units will accomplish sufficient planning to ensure successful mission accomplishment. Units will maintain facilities where all information and materials required for mission planning are available. **(T-3)**

2.2.4. Unit commanders and ACD-CCs will ensure crews have sufficient time and resources to accomplish crew mission planning and mission briefing. Units will ensure other activities, such as recurring academic training, training device periods, additional duties, etc., do not interfere with time allotted for mission planning and crew mission briefing. **(T-3)**

2.3. Mission Data Cards (MDC)

2.3.1. Squadron-generated MDCs should be used if they contain the necessary information for the type of mission being executed. At a minimum, required items are:

2.3.1.1. Tasking Order and line number. **(T-3)**

2.3.1.2. Crew line-up. **(T-3)**

2.3.1.3. Call sign. **(T-3)**

2.3.1.4. Network. **(T-3)**

2.3.1.5. Communication plan. **(T-3)**

2.3.1.6. Vulnerability/operating window. **(T-3)**

2.3.1.7. Deconfliction plan. **(T-3)**

2.4. Briefings

2.4.1. ACD-CC is responsible for presenting a briefing to promote safe and effective missions. All crewmembers must attend the mission brief unless previously coordinated with the squadron director of operations (SQ/DO). **(T-3)**

2.4.2. ACD-CC must plan adequate time to discuss required briefing items commensurate with the complexity of the mission and operator capabilities. **(T-3)**

2.4.2.1. Any item published in MAJCOM/Numbered Air Force (NAF)/wing/group/squadron standards or AFIs and understood by all participants may be briefed as "standard." **(T-3)**.

2.4.3. Briefings must start at least one half-hour prior to scheduled mission execution. **(T-3)**

2.4.4. Briefing Guides. Briefing guides will be used by the lead briefer with a reference list of items which may apply to particular missions. Units may augment these guides as necessary. Items may be briefed in any sequence, provided all minimum requirements listed in this AFI and other local directives and guidance are addressed. **(T-3)**.

2.4.5. All briefings will include as a minimum:

2.4.5.1. Risk Management. **(T-3)**

2.4.5.2. Go/No-Go status. **(T-3)**

2.4.5.3. Mission priorities and objectives. **(T-3)**

2.4.5.4. Crew Line-up. **(T-3)**

2.4.5.5. Rollback, Contingency Plans (Abort Criteria). **(T-3)**

2.4.5.6. Push times, Route, Deconfliction, Environment, Time Over Target/Terrain (TOT/T), & Re-attacks. **(T-3)**

2.4.5.7. Significant rules (e.g., Special Instructions (SPINs), Training rules, Rules of Engagement (ROE)). **(T-3)**

2.4.5.8. Roles and responsibilities of each crewmember. **(T-3)**

2.4.5.9. Weapon system and facility status. **(T-3)**

2.4.5.10. Intel support will brief the intelligence portion. **(T-3)**

2.4.6. Anyone not attending the mission brief must receive, at a minimum, an overview of the mission objectives, their roles and responsibilities and emergency procedures (EP) prior to step. **(T-3)**

2.4.7. Unbriefed missions/events will not be executed. **(T-3)**

2.4.8. Positional Changeover Brief. For operational needs, the crew may be required to brief an oncoming crewmember. When required, a positional changeover briefing with the oncoming crewmember will be delivered IAW checklist(s) and applicable directives. **(T-3)**

2.4.9. Alternate Mission Briefs. Brief planned alternate missions to be conducted if the originally planned and briefed mission is cancelled/aborted or the mission was No-Go for some reason (e.g., equipment malfunction, etc.). **(T-3)**

2.4.9.1. If the alternate mission does not parallel the planned mission, brief the specific mission elements that are different. **(T-3)**

2.4.9.2. Mission elements may be modified and briefed after start of execution as long as mission safety is not compromised. Mission Commanders will ensure changes are acknowledged by all crewmembers. **(T-3)**

2.4.9.3. Unbriefed missions/events will not be executed. **(T-3)**

2.4.10. Multiple Sortie Days. If all crewmembers attend an initial mission brief, the ACD-CC on subsequent missions need brief only those items that changed from the previous mission(s). **(T-3)**

Chapter 3

NORMAL OPERATING PROCEDURES

3.1. Pre-Mission Arrival Times. The ACD-CC, in coordination with the DO, may adjust crew report time to meet mission requirements. Crew report times will allow sufficient time to accomplish all pre-mission activities. **(T-3)**

3.1.1. Pre-Planned Missions. For pre-planned missions, crew report times are no later than one hour prior to execution to allow sufficient time to accomplish all pre-mission activities. **(T-3)**

3.1.2. Same Day Planned Missions. For sorties not pre-planned, crew will use a 3.5 hour show time prior to mission execution. **(T-3)**

3.1.3. Mission Planning Cell (MPC). If an MPC is utilized, the SQ/DO or MPC Chief (MPCC) will determine the show time. **(T-3)**

3.2. Pre-Mission Duties. Prior to scheduled mission execution, crew should only be scheduled for duties related to the mission, regardless of duty day. Example: Crewmember is scheduled for a sortie from 8 am – 12 pm; crewmember duty day is scheduled from 7 am – 3 pm. Prior to mission execution, crewmember performs pre-mission duties (e.g., planning, briefing, etc.). After the mission debrief, crew is released to perform other/additional duties. **(T-3)**

3.3. Go/No Go. SQ/CC will implement the Go/No-Go program to ensure individual crew members are current, qualified, and/or adequately supervised to perform operations and have reviewed CIF Volume 1, Part B prior to conducting operations. Crew members will not operate the weapon system until the Go/No-Go is accomplished and verified. **(T-3)**

3.3.1. SQ/CC will designate in writing those individuals responsible for accomplishing the daily Go/No-Go verification for all crew members performing mission duties for that day. Note: The Go/No-Go shall not be performed by individuals performing crew mission duties for that day. **(T-3)**

3.3.2. Designated individuals will verify, document, and sign off on the Go/No-Go status prior to releasing crew members for any scheduled mission. Go/No-Go accomplishment will be acknowledged during the mission pre-brief as an essential briefing item. The unit will maintain documentation of the Go/No-Go accomplishment and verification for one year. **(T-3)**

3.3.2.1. If the Go/No-Go verification is automated, unit operating instructions will include backup procedures to permit Go/No-Go verification when the relevant information system is unavailable. **(T-3)**

3.3.3. At a minimum, the unit Go/No-Go process will verify the following for all crew members, to include instructors and evaluators, scheduled to perform crew duties:

3.3.3.1. Qualification/certification of each scheduled crew member IAW AFI 17-2ACD Volumes 1 and 2 for the crew position, mission, and duties they are scheduled to perform. Note: Crewmembers not qualified/certified will be in training status and will require instructor or evaluator supervision to conduct crew duties. **(T-3)**

3.3.3.2. Currency and proficiency of each scheduled crew member IAW AFI 17-2ACD Volume 1 for the crew position, mission, and duties they are scheduled to perform. Note: Crewmembers not current in the crew position and/or mission will require instructor supervision to conduct crew duties until regaining currency. **(T-3)**

3.3.3.3. Currency of each crewmember on the review of all CIF Volume 1, Part B read file items. Note: An initial review and certification of all volumes will be accomplished prior to an individual's first training or operational mission. Assigned or attached crew members on extensive absence from conducting missions (90 days or more) will accomplish a complete review of all volumes prior to operations. **(T-3)**

3.4. Crew Information File (CIF)/Crew Bulletins (CB). Crewmembers will review CIF/CBs before all missions, and update the CIF currency record with the latest CIF item number, date, and crewmember's initials. **(T-3)**

3.4.1. Electronic signatures or sign-off may be used on CIFs. **(T-3)**

3.4.2. Crewmembers delinquent in CIF review or joining a mission enroute will receive a CIF update from a primary crewmember on the mission. **(T-3)**

3.4.3. Items in the CB may include local procedures and policies concerning equipment and personnel generally not included in any other publications. **(T-3)**

3.5. Unit-Developed Checklist/Local Crew Aids.

3.5.1. Locally developed checklists and crew aids may be used and will, at a minimum, include the following:

3.5.1.1. Emergency action checklists and communication-out information. **(T-3)**

3.5.1.2. Other information as deemed necessary by the unit (i.e., local training diagrams, and local area maps of sufficient detail to provide situational awareness on area boundaries). **(T-3)**

3.5.2. Unit Stan/Eval will maintain the listing of current and authorized checklists, crew aids, etc. in the CIF library. **(T-3)**

3.6. Forms and Logs. The Master Station Log (MSL) is the unit's official record of events that occurred during operations or training. The MSL is intended to maintain an accurate and detailed record of all significant events pertaining to operations occurring during each sortie. The ACD-CC is responsible for documenting significant events/crew actions in the MSL. **(T-3)**

3.6.1. ACD-CC is responsible for content, accuracy, and timeliness of all inputs to mission-related information management portals/collaborative information sharing environments IAW applicable directives, tasking, and policy. **(T-3)**

3.7. Required Equipment/Publications. All crewmembers will have all equipment and publications required for mission execution. These may be maintained and carried electronically provided operable viewing and printing capability exists through-out mission execution. OGV will maintain the list of required equipment/publication items. **(T-3)**

3.7.1. The ACD-CC is responsible for ensuring contents and mission readiness of the Deployment Case, Password Binder, and other critical documentation required for mission execution. **(T-3)**

3.7.2. Required equipment includes, but is not limited to personal accounts, passwords, password grids, all required logins, orders, etc. **(T-3)**

3.8. Operations Check (Ops Check).

3.8.1. ACD-CC's will perform Ops Checks at initial check-in, during times of authentication, and as required during sortie period based on mission triggers and requirements. **(T-3)**

3.8.2. Crews will, at a minimum, check the following items during Ops Checks: route, environment, verification of access, and terrain. **(T-3)**

3.9. On Station/Off Station. Crews will be prepared for mission execution and are expected to be on station at the beginning of the time over target/terrain (TOT/T), and must be off station by the end of the TOT/T, unless there are circumstances beyond crew control. **(T-3)**

3.9.1. A crewmember is considered to be "on-station" when conducting operations on tasked terrain and targets. A crewmember is considered to be "off-station" once operations on tasked terrain and targets have concluded." Rationale: clearly articulate On/Off Station delineations. **(T-3)**.

3.9.2. A crew is considered to be "off station" when a crewmember maneuvers off the assigned task and is no longer assigned to the terrain/target. Egress may be required to leave tasked terrain and/or targets. "Off station" indicates that the crew is not in position or no longer performing assigned tasks. **(T-3)**

3.10. Vulnerability (VUL) Window. Crews are bounded by the VUL window. Deviations from the assigned VUL window must be coordinated through the ACD-CC and approved by the tasking authority. **(T-3)**

3.11. Abort/Knock-it-off. A tactical commander may declare a knock-it-off (training use only) or abort (cease action/event/mission). **(T-3)**

3.12. Dynamic Targeting. Ad hoc and/or emerging target tasking can occur. During tasked missions, an operator may identify and report something that may require ad hoc or dynamic targeting/retasking. Dynamic retasking allows modification of the mission to support changing mission objectives. This includes everything from retasking the operator within the mission requirements to an entirely new mission that is added to the daily tasking order. Retasking is accomplished through the tasking authority. **(T-3)**

3.13. Communications and Crew Coordination. Recorded crew communications are official communications and all crews should be aware they have no expectation of privacy. **(T-3)**

3.13.1. Sterile Ops Floor. Limit conversation through official communication channels to that which is essential for crew coordination and mission accomplishment. **(T-3)**

3.13.2. Advisory Calls. The operator performing the execution will periodically announce their intentions during the critical checkpoints/phases of operations and when circumstances require deviating from normal procedures. **(T-3)**

3.13.3. Common brevity codes may be found in the current SPINs. **(T-3)**

3.13.4. Communications.

3.13.4.1. Mission execution requires at least one method of communication for all operations. **(T-3)**

3.13.4.2. The ACD-CC is responsible for developing and briefing the communication plan. **(T-3)**

3.13.4.3. Communications planning is performed to determine who should talk, when and via what medium. **(T-3)**

3.13.4.4. The ACD-CC will ensure a designated crewmember monitors all primary comms unless otherwise directed, during all phases of operations. **(T-3)**

3.13.4.5. An example Communications Planning Guide is included in Attachment 4.

3.14. Mission Report (MISREP). The ACD-CC is responsible for providing timely, accurate, and correctly formatted reports to tasking authority. **(T-3)**

3.14.1. Tasking authorities, future missions and debriefs rely on accurate, timely MISREPs. All MISREPs will be completed IAW tasking authority guidance.

3.14.2. Complete the MISREP once the crew completes a mission or specific mission phase IAW guidance/tasking.

3.14.3. The ACD-CC is responsible for reviewing the MISREP for accuracy and completeness and submission to tasking authority. **(T-3)**

3.14.4. Each member, section, or element lead on the crew is responsible for providing the appropriate data regarding their mission area. **(T-3)**

3.14.5. Units may develop local procedures/templates to ensure standardization of reporting. **(T-3)**

3.15. Crew Changeover. Direct crew changeover only applies if crews are performing 24/7 operations. If 24/7 operations are not occurring then the crew changeover briefing will be incorporated into the next day's pre-mission briefing. Crew members from the off-going and on-coming sorties during a multi-sortie day will participate in a crew changeover briefing. At a minimum, the changeover will include all items previously identified for the pre-mission briefing. **(T-3)**

3.16. Debriefing.

3.16.1. All missions will be debriefed. **(T-3)**

3.16.2. The ACD-CC is responsible for leading the crew debriefs. **(T-3)**

3.16.3. Debriefs will cover all aspects of the mission (planning, briefing and execution) and ensure all participants receive feedback through the development of Lessons Learned (LL) and Learning Points (LP). **(T-3)**

3.16.4. Debrief will cover crewmember responsibilities, deconfliction, tactical employment priorities and task management. **(T-3)**

3.16.5. ACD-CC will review the record of all tactical portions of the sortie to assess members' effectiveness. **(T-3)**

3.16.6. An example debriefing guide can be found in Attachment 3.

3.17. Post Mission Duties.

3.17.1. Each crewmember will complete any further tasks in relation to the current mission deemed necessary by the ACD-CC. **(T-3)**

3.17.2. Ops Floor Cleanliness. It is the ACD-CC and/or Mission Commander's (MC) responsibility to ensure the ops floor is clean and orderly after a mission. All crewmembers are responsible for removing or stowing their personal and professional items prior to departing the floor. **(T-3)**

Chapter 4

CREW DUTIES, RESPONSIBILITIES, AND PROCEDURES

4.1. The ACD-CC is responsible for the safe, effective conduct of operations. The crew is responsible to the ACD-CC for the successful accomplishment of all activities. ACD-CC responsibilities include:

4.1.1. Managing crew resources and safe mission accomplishment. **(T-3)**

4.1.2. Welfare of the crew. **(T-3)**

4.1.3. Ensuring that any portion of the operation affecting mission accomplishment is coordinated with the tasking authority. **(T-3)**

4.1.4. Ensuring the unit-developed risk management decision matrix is completed prior to mission briefing. **(T-3)**

4.2. Crew Stations. Operators shall be in their seats on the operations floor during the critical checkpoints/phases of execution. Crewmembers will notify the ACD-CC prior to departing their duty station. **(T-3)**

4.3. Crew Duties. Crewmembers are responsible for successful sortie completion and for the safe, effective use of the weapon system. A crew brief will be accomplished before each mission execution to ensure an understanding of all aspects of the mission. **(T-3)**

4.4. Crew Positions.

4.4.1. ACD Crew Commander (ACD-CC). Serves as the command authority for ACD crew operations and provides command oversight for operations floor personnel as well as enforcing policies and procedures to ensure successful mission accomplishment.

4.4.2. ACD Operations Controller (ACD-OC). Conducts mission control for ACD weapon system management and operations. Assists the ACD-CC as the command authority for ACD crew operations and provides command oversight for operations floor personnel as well as enforcing policies and procedures to ensure successful mission accomplishment.

4.4.3. Air Force Cyberspace Defense Operator (ACD-O). Operates the ACD Alert mission conducting enduring enterprise-wide, friendly and adversary force monitoring, and alerting for the intended purpose of nominating targets for further action (i.e., intercepting and mitigating malicious adversaries/activity).

4.4.4. Host-based Security (ACD-O/HBS). Operates the ACD host-based cyberspace alert capability through enduring NIPRNet and SIPRNet alert to nominate targets for further action.

4.4.5. Defensive Counter Cyberspace (ACD-O/DCC) Qualified to execute interdiction, strike, surveillance, reconnaissance, and QRF missions on specified terrain to prevent targets from executing properly, eliminate targets, identify and nominate targets, or characterize targets, respectively.

4.4.6. Incident Response ACD-O/IR. Executes surveillance missions after the detection of an emerging target to characterize target(s); confirming or invalidating target(s) providing amplifying targeting information for follow-on forces.

4.5. Crew Manning. Mission crew manning may vary by the type of mission; SQ/DO may tailor crew manning to meet operational requirements. See table 4.1 for minimum required crew.

Table 4.1. Standard Crew Line-Up.

	ACD-CC	ACD-OC	ACD-O	HBS	DCC	IR	Min Crew
Min required crew	1	1	3	1	1	1	8

4.6. Crew Qualification. Each person assigned as a primary crewmember must be qualified or in training status for that crew position, mission, and weapon system. Those crewmembers in a training status will accomplish weapon system operations and/or duties only under the supervision of a qualified instructor. **(T-3)**

4.6.1. Basic mission capable (BMC) crewmembers may perform primary crew duties on any training mission. The unit commander must determine the readiness of each BMC crewmember to perform primary crew duties. **(T-3)**

4.6.2. Mission ready (MR) crewmembers may perform primary crew duties in any position in which they maintain qualification, certification, currency and proficiency. **(T-3)**

4.6.3. Non-current or Unqualified crew may perform crew duties only on designated training or evaluation missions under the supervision of a qualified instructor/evaluator. **(T-3)**

4.7. New/Modified Equipment and/or Capabilities. Crewmembers not qualified and/or certified in the operation of new or modified equipment and/or weapon system capabilities will not operate that equipment or perform any duties associated with that equipment or capability(ies) unless under the supervision of a current and qualified instructor of like specialty and otherwise specified by MAJCOM guidance. **(T-3)**

4.8. Crew Rest/Duty Period/Sortie Duration. Crew rest, crew duty period and crew augmentation will be IAW all applicable guidance with the following additional guidance:

4.8.1. Crew Rest. Crew rest is a minimum 12-hour non-duty period before the duty period begins and is intended to ensure the crew member is adequately rested before performing a mission or mission-related duties. Crew rest is free time, and includes time for meals, transportation and rest. Rest is defined as a condition that allows an individual the opportunity to sleep. Each crew member is individually responsible for ensuring they obtain sufficient rest during crew rest periods. **(T-3)**

4.8.2. Exceptions to the 12-Hour Minimum Crew Rest Period. For continuous operations when basic crew duty periods are greater than 12 but less than 14 hours, subsequent crew rest may be reduced proportionally to a minimum of 10 hours to maintain a 24-hour work/rest schedule with unit commander approval. **(T-3)**

4.8.2.1. Continuous operations mean three or more consecutive sorties of at least 12 hours duration separated by minimum crew rest. **(T-3)**

4.8.2.2. The crew rest exception shall only be used for contingency/surge operations and not for scheduling conveniences. **(T-3)**

4.8.3. Duty Period. The maximum crew duty period shall not exceed 12 hours unless approved by the OG/CC. **(T-3)**.

4.8.4. Sortie. For planning purposes, the average sortie duration (ASD) is eight (8) hours. (T-3)

4.9. Crew Scheduling. Scheduling mission crews will be accomplished IAW crew rest limitations provided in this AFI. Units will make every effort to ensure compliance. **(T-3)**

4.9.1. Units will attempt to provide all crew members as stable a schedule as possible. A standard rotation for 24/7 crews should be utilized to enhance performance. **(T-3)**

4.9.2. Schedulers will publish, post, and monitor schedules for the crew force and initiate changes to the schedules based on tracking of qualifications, certifications, restrictions and other factors as required to meet mission objectives. **(T-3)**

4.9.2.1. An operations scheduler will ensure a crew member on leave or temporary duty (TDY) is notified if a schedule change places or changes an event on their schedule during the first 72 hours after their scheduled return. **(T-3)**

4.9.2.2. Schedulers will notify crewmembers of changes as soon as practical after the change is official, but not later than 12 hours prior to the scheduled event time. **(T-3)**

WILLIAM J. BENDER, Lt Gen, USAF
Chief of Information Dominance and Chief
Information Officer

Attachment 1

GLOSSARY OF REFERENCES AND SUPPORTING INFORMATION

References

24 AF, AFCYBER and JFHQ-C AFCYBER Tactical Mission Planning, Briefing and Debriefing Guide, 16 Dec 15

AFPD 17-2, *Cyberspace Operations*, 12 April 2016

AFI 17-202 V3, *Cyberspace Operations and Procedures*, 15 February 2014

AFI 17-2ACD Volume 1, *Air Force Cyberspace Defense (ACD) Training*

AFI 17-2ACD Volume 2, *Air Force Cyberspace Defense (ACD) Standardization and Evaluation*

AFI 33-360, *Publications and Forms Management*, 1 December 2015

AFI 11-215, *USAF Flight Manuals Program (FMP)*, 22 December 2008

AFMAN 33-363, *Management of Records*, 1 March 2008

AFTTP 3-1.ACD

AFCYBER & JFHQ-C AFCYBER Tactical Mission Planning, Briefing and Debriefing Guide

AFTTP 3-1.General Planning

AFTTP 3-1.Threat Guide Chapter 13

USAFWS "A Mission Commander's Handbook," Captain Brad J. Bashore, 13 Dec 2008

USAFWS "ME3C-(PC)2: A Problem Solving Methodology," Captain Raymond L. Daniel, 13 June 2009

USAFWS "Methodology of the Debrief," Captain Robert L. Brown, 10 June 2006

MULTI-SERVICE BREVITY CODES, AFTTP 3-2.5, September 2014

Flash Bulletin (FB) 12-12, *Defensive Cyberspace Operations-Tactical Coordinator*

FB 14-19, *Defensive Cyber Operations Large Force Employment Considerations*

Prescribed Forms

None

Adopted Forms

AF Form 847, *Recommendation for Change of Publication*

AFTO Form 781, *ARMS Crew/Mission Data Document*

Abbreviations and Acronyms

ACD— Air Force Cyberspace Defense

ACD-CC - Crew Commander

ACD-O - AF Cyberspace Defense Operator

ACD/OC— AF Cyberspace Defense Operations Controller

AF— Air Force

AFCYBER— Air Forces Cyber

AFPD— Air Force Policy Directive

AFI— Air Force Instruction

AFMAN— Air Force Manual

AFRC— Air Force Reserve Command

AFRIMS— Air Force Records Information Management System

AFSPC— Air Force Space Command

AFTTP— Air Force Tactics, Techniques and Procedures

ANG— Air National Guard

ASD— Average Sortie Duration

BCQ— Basic Crew Qualification

BMC— Basic Mission Capable

CB—Crew Bulletin

CIF— Crew Information File

CT— Continuation Training

DCC— Defensive Counter Cyberspace

DMC— Deputy Mission Commander

DPMCC— Deputy Mission Planning Cell Chief

DO— Director of Operations

EP— Emergency Procedures

FB— Flash Bulletin

HBS - Host—Based Security

IAW— In Accordance With

IRO— Incident Response

JFHQ-C - Joint Forces Headquarters-Cyber

LL— Lesson Learned

LP— Learning Point

MAJCOM— Major Command

MC— Mission Commander

MDC— Mission Data Card

MISREP— Mission Report

MPC— Mission Planning Cell

MPCC— Mission Planning Cell Chief

MR— Mission Ready

NAF— Numbered Air Force

NC— Non-current

OG— Operations Group

OGV— Standardization and Evaluation

OPR— Office of Primary Responsibility

PAA— Preapproved Actions

PC— Package Commander

PIC— Person in Charge

QRF— Quick Reaction Force

RDS— Records Disposition Schedule

ROE— Rules of Engagement

SCAR—Strike Control and Reconnaissance

SOP— Standard Operating Procedures

SPINS— Special Instructions

SQ— Squadron

TOT/T— Time over Target/Terrain

TRP— Tactical Reconnaissance Package

UNQ— Unqualified

USAF— United States Air Force

VUL— Vulnerability

Terms

Air Force Cyberspace Defense Operator (ACD—O) – An individual who operates the ACD Alert mission conducting enduring enterprise-wide, friendly and adversary force monitoring, and alerting for the intended purpose of nominating targets for further action (i.e., intercepting and mitigating malicious adversaries/activity).

Average Sortie Duration (ASD)— Converts sorties to flying/execution hours and vice versa. MAJCOM/A2/3/6TB and AFSPC/A2/3/6T use the unit's last programmed ASD when initially determining execution/flying hour's programs for the current and future years. Units will update ASD annually to reflect the unit's best estimate of the optimum sortie duration after considering historical experiences, changes in missions, deployments, etc. The formula to calculate ASD is ASD=# of weapon system hours employed divided by number of sorties.

Basic Mission Capable (BMC)— A crewmember who satisfactorily completed IQT and MQT to perform the unit's basic operational missions, but does not maintain MR/CMR status. Crewmember accomplishes training required to remain familiarized in all and may be qualified and proficient in some of the primary missions of their weapon system BMC requirements. These crewmembers may also maintain special mission qualification.

Basic Cybercrew Qualification (BCQ)— A crew member who has satisfactorily completed IQT. The crewmember will carry BCQ only until completion of MQT. BCQ crewmembers will not perform RCP-tasked events or sorties without instructor crewmembers.

Campaign— A series of related major operations aimed at achieving strategic and operational objectives within a given time and space.

Certification— Designation of an individual by the certifying official as completing required training and/or evaluation and being capable of performing a specific duty.

Composite Force Training (CFT)— Scenarios employing multiple units of the same or different weapon systems types, each under the direction of its own package leader, performing the same or different roles. Only one event may be logged per mission.

Continuation Training (CT)— Training which provides crew members the volume, frequency, and mix of training necessary to maintain currency and proficiency in the assigned qualification level.

Core Mission Sortie— Operational mission actions or training scenario profiles relating to the unit's DOC statement requirements.

Core Mission— Operational mission actions or training scenario profiles relating to the unit's DOC statement requirements. The base mechanism used to achieve missions is sorties.

Crew Commander (ACD-CC)— An individual who serves as the command authority for ACD crew operations and provides command oversight for operations floor personnel as well as enforcing policies and procedures to ensure successful mission accomplishment.

Crew Information File (CIF)— A collection of publications and material determined by the MAJCOM and unit as necessary for day-to-day operations.

Crew Position Indicator (CPI)— A code used to manage crew positions to ensure a high state of readiness is maintained with available resources.

Crew— Also referred to as crew members; a group of individuals who conduct cyberspace operations or computer network exploitation and are typically assigned to a specific weapon system.

Currency— A measure of how frequently and/or recently a task is completed. Currency requirements should ensure the average crew member maintains a minimum level of proficiency in a specific event.

Cyber (adj.)— Of or pertaining to the cyberspace environment, capabilities, plans, or operations.

Cyberspace Operations— The employment of cyberspace capabilities where the primary purpose is to achieve objectives in or through cyberspace.

Cyberspace— A global domain within the information environment consisting of the interdependent network of information technology infrastructures and resident data, including the Internet, telecommunications networks, computer systems, and embedded processors and controllers.

Defensive Counter Cyber (DCC)— Qualified to execute interdiction, strike, surveillance, reconnaissance, and quick reaction (QRF) missions on specified terrain to prevent targets from executing properly, eliminate targets, identify and nominate targets, or characterize targets, respectively.

Deviation— An action not in compliance with current procedures, directives, or regulations. Action(s) performed out of sequence due to unusual or extenuating circumstances are not considered a deviation. In some cases, momentary deviations may be acceptable; however, cumulative deviations will be considered in determining the overall qualification level for an evaluation.

Event— An item that occurs or is encountered that initiates a process requiring a set of tasks to be accomplished. Multiple events may be completed and logged during a sortie (be it operational sortie or a training sortie) unless specifically excluded elsewhere in this instruction.

Experienced Crewmember (EXP)— A crewmember who meets the requirements dictated within the weapon system specific volumes.

Host—based Security (HBS) - Operates the ACD host-based cyberspace alert capability through enduring alert on NIPRNet and SIPRNet to nominate targets for further action.

Incident Response (IRO)— Executes surveillance missions after the detection of an emerging target to characterize target(s); confirm or invalidate target(s) and provide amplifying targeting information for follow-on forces.

Instructor— An experienced individual qualified to instruct other individuals in mission area academics and positional duties. Instructors will be qualified appropriately to the level of the training they provide.

Internal Active Defense— The synchronized, real-time capability to discover, detect, analyze, and mitigate threats and vulnerabilities to defend networks and systems.

Mission Ready/Combat Mission Ready (MR/CMR))— A crew member who satisfactorily completed IQT and MQT, and maintains certification, currency and proficiency in the command or unit mission.

Mission— An operation with an intended purpose, by a unit and/or units with relevant capability and preponderance of capacity. The base mechanism used to achieve mission objectives is sorties. Missions may require multiple sorties from multiple units to accomplish the mission's objectives.

Non-current (NC) or Unqualified (UNQ)— Crew members who may perform crew duties only on designated training or evaluation missions under the supervision of a qualified instructor/evaluator.

Off Station— When a force package maneuvers off the assigned task and is no longer assigned to the terrain/target. Egress may be required to leave tasked terrain and/or targets. Indicates that crewmember(s) is not in position or no longer performing assigned tasks.

On Station— When the cyberspace operation commences on tasked terrain and targets. Ingress/Egress may be required to reach tasked terrain and/or targets. Plan accordingly for mission execution success. On station indicates crew reached assigned TOT/T.

Operations Controller (COC)—The individual who serves as the command authority for ACD crew operations and provides command oversight for operations floor personnel as well as enforcing policies and procedures to ensure successful mission accomplishment.

Qualification— Designation of an individual by the unit commander as having completed required training and evaluation and being capable of performing a specific duty.

Ready Cybercrew Program (RCP)— The formal CT program that provides the baseline for squadrons to use in developing a realistic training program to meet all DOC statement tasked requirements as well as specific NAF mission prioritization. RCP defines the minimum required mix of annual sorties, simulator missions, and training events crew must accomplish to sustain mission readiness. These programs have clearly defined objectives and minimum standard that enhance mission accomplishment and safety. RCP sorties are tracked. To be effective, each mission must involve successfully completing a sufficient number of events applicable to that mission type, as determined by the Squadron Commander. With completion of IQT and MQT, a crewmember is trained in all the basic missions of a specific unit, unless a specific exception is provided in the weapon system-specific Volume 1. RCP applies to CMR/MR and BMC positions.

Sortie— The actions an individual weapon system takes to accomplish a mission and/or mission objective(s) within a defined start and stop period.

Target— The adversary, purposeful malicious actor code, or processes residing in blue or gray terrain. Targets include, but are not limited to, processes, code, credentials, storage, and the countering of adversary TIP designed to establish persistent access and C2.

Task— A clearly defined action or activity specifically assigned to an individual or organization that must be accomplished as imposed by an appropriate authority.

Terrain— The cyberspace area of operations where a force package is directed to conduct a sortie. Terrain is defined as Internet Protocol (IP) address, domain, or transport space within the DoDIN or AF enclave (commonly referred to as "blue" space), or commercial, contractor-owned , mission partner-owned ("grey" space) host, server, and network devices that enable C2, communication, sensing, and access capabilities.

Time Over Target/Terrain (TOT)— The exact timing requested by the tactical commander, directed by the tasking authority, or specified in the tasking order to prosecute a mission. The TOT is based on the available VUL window (can be an enduring or time-sensitive requirement) and must be executed within the VUL window; authorization for a TOT outside a VUL window can only be authorized by the tasking authority.

Total ASD Time— Total time for all sorties flown in military service to include student time. Time accumulated must be in the crew member's current rating.

Upgrade Training— Training needed to qualify for crew position of additional responsibility for a specific weapon system (e.g., special mission qualifications).

Vulnerability (VUL) Window— A window of opportunity and direction for a tactical commander to conduct operations. A VUL Window is bounded (start by/finish by) to provide a tactical commander the authorized and suspensed timing available to plan and prosecute a mission. Deviations from the assigned VUL Window must be approved by the tasking authority.

Weapon System— A combination of one or more weapons with all related equipment, materials, services, personnel, and means of delivery and deployment (if applicable) required for self-sufficiency.

Attachment 2

DEBRIEF

Figure A2.1. Debrief Presentation Format:

- ☐ Classification
- ☐ ROE
- ☐ Admin/Alibis
- ☐ Objectives
- ☐ Planning
- ☐ Execution
- ☐ Big Rocks
- ☐ DFPs
- ☐ Lessons Learned
- ☐ Assessments

Attachment 3

COMMUNICATIONS PLANNING GUIDE

Figure A3.1. Communications Planning Guide.

OBJECTIVE: Develop a simple plan to specify who should talk, when, and via what medium.

- ☐ Check orders and SPINs, ROEs, Preapproved Actions (PAAs), etc. for applicable:
    - ○ Comm standards
    - ○ Check-in procedures
    - ○ Code words and brevity terms
    - ○ Authentication
    - ○ Other comm procedures applicable to the mission

- ☐ Comm plan specifics:
    - ○ Weapon system/location operations
    - ○ Sortie period/timing
    - ○ Chat rooms/channels (i.e. single chat room vs multiple chat rooms)
        - ▪ Specific server names/URLs/IPs as needed
        - ▪ Chat room assignments
        - ▪ Room purposes (execution vs planning)
    - ○ Multi-level security considerations
    - ○ Triggers/contracts for transitioning between primary and backup comm

- ☐ Ensure the COMM plan is delivered to all mission partners via Coord Card
    - ○ Maintain version control (e.g. "Current as of DATE/TIME")

Cybersecurity Titles Published by 4th Watch Publishing Co.

NIST SP 1800-4a & 4b Mobile Device Security: Cloud and Hybrid Builds
NIST SP 1800-4c Mobile Device Security: Cloud and Hybrid Builds
NIST SP 1800-5 IT Asset Management: Financial Services
NIST SP 1800-6 Domain Name Systems-Based Electronic Mail Security
NIST SP 1800-7 Situational Awareness for Electric Utilities
NIST SP 1800-8 Securing Wireless Infusion Pumps
NIST SP 1800-9a & 9b Access Rights Management for the Financial Services Sector
NIST SP 1800-9c Access Rights Management for the Financial Services Sector - How To Guide
NIST SP 1800-11a & 11b Data Integrity Recovering from Ransomware and Other Destructive Events
NIST SP 1800-11c Data Integrity Recovering from Ransomware and Other Destructive Events - How To Guide
NIST SP 1800-12 Derived Personal Identity Verification (PIV) Credentials
NISTIR 7298 R2 Glossary of Key Information Security Terms
NISTIR 7316 Assessment of Access Control Systems
NISTIR 7497 Security Architecture Design Process for Health Information Exchanges (HIEs)
NISTIR 7511 R4 V1.2 Security Content Automation Protocol (SCAP) Version 1.2 Validation Program Test Requirements
NISTIR 7628 R1 Vol 1 Guidelines for Smart Grid Cybersecurity - Architecture, and High-Level Requirements
NISTIR 7628 R1 Vol 2 Guidelines for Smart Grid Cybersecurity - Privacy and the Smart Grid
NISTIR 7628 R1 Vol 3 Guidelines for Smart Grid Cybersecurity - Supportive Analyses and References
NISTIR 7756 CAESARS Framework Extension: An Enterprise Continuous Monitoring Technical Refer
NISTIR 7788 Security Risk Analysis of Enterprise Networks Using Probabilistic Attack Graphs
NISTIR 7823 Advanced Metering Infrastructure Smart Meter Upgradeability Test Framework
NISTIR 7874 Guidelines for Access Control System Evaluation Metrics
NISTIR 7904 Trusted Geolocation in the Cloud: Proof of Concept Implementation
NISTIR 7924 Reference Certificate Policy
NISTIR 7987 Policy Machine: Features, Architecture, and Specification
NISTIR 8006 NIST Cloud Computing Forensic Science Challenges
NISTIR 8011 Vol 1 Automation Support for Security Control Assessments
NISTIR 8011 Vol 2 Automation Support for Security Control Assessments
NISTIR 8040 Measuring the Usability and Security of Permuted Passwords on Mobile Platforms
NISTIR 8053 De-Identification of Personal Information
NISTIR 8054 NSTIC Pilots: Catalyzing the Identity Ecosystem
NISTIR 8055 Derived Personal Identity Verification (PIV) Credentials (DPC) Proof of Concept Research
NISTIR 8060 Guidelines for the Creation of Interoperable Software Identification (SWID) Tags
NISTIR 8062 Introduction to Privacy Engineering and Risk Management in Federal Systems
NISTIR 8074 Vol 1 & Vol 2 Strategic U.S. Government Engagement in International Standardization to Achieve U.S. Objectives for Cybersecurity
NISTIR 8080 Usability and Security Considerations for Public Safety Mobile Authentication
NISTIR 8089 An Industrial Control System Cybersecurity Performance Testbed
NISTIR 8112 Attribute Metadata - Draft
NISTIR 8135 Identifying and Categorizing Data Types for Public Safety Mobile Applications
NISTIR 8138 Vulnerability Description Ontology (VDO)
NISTIR 8144 Assessing Threats to Mobile Devices & Infrastructure
NISTIR 8151 Dramatically Reducing Software Vulnerabilities
NISTIR 8170 The Cybersecurity Framework
NISTIR 8176 Security Assurance Requirements for Linux Application Container Deployments
NISTIR 8179 Criticality Analysis Process Model
NISTIR 8183 Cybersecurity Framework Manufacturing Profile
NISTIR 8192 Enhancing Resilience of the Internet and Communications Ecosystem
Whitepaper Cybersecurity Framework Manufacturing Profile
Whitepaper NIST Framework for Improving Critical Infrastructure Cybersecurity
Whitepaper Challenging Security Requirements for US Government Cloud Computing Adoption
FIPS PUBS 140-2 Security Requirements for Cryptographic Modules
FIPS PUBS 140-2 Annex A Approved Security Functions
FIPS PUBS 140-2 Annex B Approved Protection Profiles
FIPS PUBS 140-2 Annex C Approved Random Number Generators
FIPS PUBS 140-2 Annex D Approved Key Establishment Techniques
FIPS PUBS 180-4 Secure Hash Standard (SHS)
FIPS PUBS 186-4 Digital Signature Standard (DSS)
FIPS PUBS 197 Advanced Encryption Standard (AES)
FIPS PUBS 198-1 The Keyed-Hash Message Authentication Code (HMAC)
FIPS PUBS 199 Standards for Security Categorization of Federal Information and Information Systems
FIPS PUBS 200 Minimum Security Requirements for Federal Information and Information Systems
FIPS PUBS 201-2 Personal Identity Verification (PIV) of Federal Employees and Contractors
FIPS PUBS 202 SHA-3 Standard: Permutation-Based Hash and Extendable-Output Functions

DHS Study DHS Study on Mobile Device Security

OMB A-130 / FISMA OMB A-130/Federal Information Security Modernization Act
GAO Federal Information System Controls Audit Manual

DoD	
UFC 3-430-11	Boiler Control Systems
UFC 4-010-06	Cybersecurity of Facility-Related Control Systems
FC 4-141-05N	Navy and Marine Corps Industrial Control Systems Monitoring Stations
MIL-HDBK-232A	RED/BLACK Engineering-Installation Guidelines
MIL-HDBK 1195	Radio Frequency Shielded Enclosures
TM 5-601	Supervisory Control and Data Acquisition (SCADA) Systems for C4ISR Facilities
ESTCP	Facility-Related Control Systems Cybersecurity Guideline
ESTCP	Facility-Related Control Systems Ver 4.0
DoD	Self-Assessing Security Vulnerabilities & Risks of Industrial Controls
DoD	Program Manager's Guidebook for Integrating the Cybersecurity Risk Management Framework (RMF) into the System Acquisition Lifecycle
DoD	Advanced Cyber Industrial Control System Tactics, Techniques, and Procedures (ACI TTP)
DoD 4140.1	Supply Chain Materiel Management Procedures
AFI 17-2NAS	Air Force Network Attack System (NAS) Volume 1, 2 & 3
AFI 10-1703	Air Force Cybercrew Volume 1, 2 & 3
AFI 17-2ACD	Air Force Cyberspace Defense (ACD) Volume 1, 2 & 3
AFI 17-2CDA	Air Force Cyberspace Defense Analysis (CDA) Volume 1, 2 & 3
AFPD 17-2	Cyberspace Operations

www.ingramcontent.com/pod-product-compliance
Lightning Source LLC
LaVergne TN
LVHW060145070326

832902LV00018B/2955